Anne

with love and

appreciation

Philip L. Calcagno

91

REACHING BEYOND YOUR GRASP

PHILIP L. CALCAGNO, M.D.

Washington Publications Inc.
Nags Head, N.C.

Published by

Washington Publications Inc.
6810 Virginia Dare Trail
Nags Head, N.C.   27959
1-800-468-4226

ISBN 0-925052-13-2

*This book is dedicated to my mother who was
not only rich in dreams,
but a master of survivorship.*

*Born Margherita Mazzola in Aidone, Sicily in 1898,
and raised without formal education, my dear
mother taught me to look forward with anticipation
to the goals of tomorrow while enjoying the savor of
the accomplished goals of today.*

Acknowledgements

Many have encouraged the writing of this book. Others collaborated with opinions. Primarily, however, the young people with whom I came in contact created the basis of this book. I always appreciate having the opportunity to help and support their needs.

I am most grateful to Mrs. Caroline Patterson whose critical eye and unrelenting editorship of the raw material on hand-written yellow pages converted words to ideas and ideas into a printed manuscript using a word processor. The research and library support was done by Dr. Leticia Tina, my associate pediatric nephrologist. I am also indebted to Mrs. Glory Cromwell for supporting and safeguarding my consultation time with the students.

It has been — and is — my good fortune to live in Washington, D.C. There, an inquisitive mind has many sources for information such as the Library of Congress, the Institute of Medicine, the National Academy of Sciences, the National Institutes of Health, the Carnegie Council on Adolescent Development, the American Board of Pediatrics, the Greater Washington Board of Trade and The Council on Competitiveness.

Mary Wolffskill, director of the Manuscript Division of the Library of Congress provided invaluable reference material. Anthony S. Cooper, Manager of the Human Development Bureau was most kind in supplying Board of Trade publications. Dr. Elena O. Nightingale of the Carnegie Council on Adolescent Development contributed the report on the lack of roles for adolescents in modern society. Norma Langley allowed me to draw on her extensive experience in journalism in preparation of this book.

I am exceedingly grateful to the members of the faculty of the Department of Pediatrics at Georgetown University School of Medicine:

Val Abbassi, M.D.
A.R. Colon, M.D.
Charles Kennedy, M.D.
Phyllis Magrab, M.D.
Joseph Novello, M.D.
Robert Shearin, M.D.
Anita Soster, Ph.D.
Dorothy Whipple, M.D.
Raoul Wientzen, M.D.

Special mention goes to Elizabeth McPherson of the Department of Nursing at Georgetown University Hospital who highlighted adolescent female role identification.

A very special note to my two daughters, Alexandra and Carla, who steered me in the right direction when I stumbled and wrecked on unfamiliar ground.

This book would not be possible without the valued support and faith of the publisher, Elizabeth Jones of WPI.

Contents

Foreword

I want to talk to today's young people, their parents and teachers because I've spent 50 years in medicine as a student, physician, pediatrician and teacher. Because of my personal and professional background, I believe I have a special message for youth who face great obstacles due to poverty, social inequity, racism and peer pressures for drug and alcohol use and sexual promiscuity.

During my long medical career, I've had a front row seat for seeing negative influences exerted on today's youth. I've watched how they affect our children's growth and development, both physically and mentally.

My perspective is heightened because although I've enjoyed success as a doctor, my beginnings were humble and my life filled with the same stumbling blocks so many young people face today.

I was born to Sicilian immigrants in a tenement apartment on the east side of Manhattan in 1918. Both my parents worked in New York's garment district. Italian was my first language and I have had difficulty all my life trying to function in American English. I've also had difficulty resisting the street-life of "Little Italy," where "speak-easies," graft and all types of vice and corruption had flourished during the "Roaring 20s" and accelerated with the hard times of the 30s.

When we moved to Brooklyn in my early teens, fortunately I brought my ethnic values with me. After a close call with the law, I learned the value of staying straight.

I had developed poor study skills and was a D student in high school because I didn't know how to study. My own lack of educational and career guidance is one of the reasons I wrote this book.

Looking back, it was absurd that I, a poor student from a poor family, should decide to go to college, enter medical school and become a doctor. But that's exactly what I did. I had strong moral support from my family, something many youths don't have today. I learned how to develop self-esteem and confidence through working.

Seeing the financial destitution of the Depression motivated me to choose a profession which would provide security for me and my family. Later I began to see that I could make a worthwhile contribution to society and gain true satisfaction from life.

Today's youth need to hear that they too can overcome whatever obstacles they face and create a better life for themselves and others. After half a century of dealing with young people and their problems, one thought rings clear:

The youth of this country must set goals, pursue their dreams and exploit to the fullest their God-given talents for tomorrow, the 21st century.

They can't do this alone. We all must help them and they must learn how to seek help. They are the foundation for all our tomorrows. By working together we can keep America an environment for hard work, fair play and success.

Introduction:
A Letter to the Youth of Our Country

If I could promise that after reading this book you could know your future, you and all your friends would want to read it. We all want to know what our future holds.

But while I can't tell what lies ahead for you, I can tell you this: you hold the key and you can decide how your life's story will be played out.

This book is written to allow you to see where you're going before you get there. You have the power to determine who and what you will be. You must decide now and make the choices that will take you down the road you want to walk.

It doesn't matter where you come from. Obstacles are hidden along every path. You will confront them and they will confront you. Whether you're rich, poor or middle class; whether you're Hispanic, Afro-American, Italo-American, Irish American, Asian American, Jewish or White Anglo-Saxon Protestant you have outward differences that separate and identify you from your peers.

If you have a strong ethnic background, as I did, you may feel the obstacles you face are insurmountable. They're not. We in America attempt to maintain our roots and yet be part of the melting pot that has made our country great. It isn't easily done. The boundaries are fixed by prejudice, ignorance and our own lack of flexibility to accept differences easily. But you're not alone. You can succeed.

All young people are at risk of failure. Some more than others. In this world, however, the keys to success are self-esteem and self-discipline. Self-motivation is your driving force.

If you've ever been homeless and suffered gnawing pangs of hunger, you've experienced a particularly powerful source of motivation. You wanted those essentials and you acted quickly and decisively to obtain them.

Sometimes it takes tragedy to make us see how much will power and stamina we have. Don't wait for tragedy to strike — life is difficult enough as it is. If you're serious about wanting your life to be a success story, start working on it now.

This book gives you the tools and information you need to make the right decisions for a successful future. Develop self-esteem and self-discipline. Challenge your mind. Build a fire in your gut. And reach beyond your grasp to a better life.

> — *Philip L. Calcagno, M.D.*
> *August 1991*

Chapter 1

Start with a Winner's Attitude

"Winning is not a sometime thing," said the great coach and achiever Vince Lombardi. "You don't win once in awhile. You don't do things right once in awhile. You do them right all the time."

Lombardi identified winning as a habit you begin to establish and continue to build. Winning is only possible if you have focus, determination and a hunger for something better.

Several keys unlock the door to a winning attitude: Hard work, discipline, risk taking, belief in a purpose, proper timing and faith.

I can't stress enough the importance of hard work in the achievement of any goal. Whether your goal is to complete your education, excel at athletics or make a lot of money, you have to be prepared to put forth effort. You will get back what you invest.

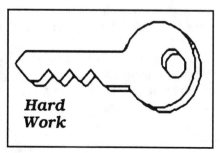

Hard Work

☐ Getting a job is vitally important in developing your winning attitude and building your self-confidence. It gives you an opportunity to become part of the adult world, to meet people and to get to know yourself better.

☐ A job encourages you to become responsible, enthusiastic and self-motivated — all character traits which will be invaluable to you for your entire life.

☐ Having a job makes you a winner. It sets you above your peers — and that strengthens your winning habit even more.

☐ A job may prepare you more for what you want to do in life than many of your classes at school.

☐ And, last but not least, a job will bring in money.

There are many ways you can earn money: bagging or stocking groceries at a supermarket; neighborhood yard work; caddying at the local golf course. Restaurants — from fine dining establishments to fast food chains — amusement parks, retail stores and other businesses offer a variety of part-time or seasonal jobs that can be filled by teenagers.

> **A job you have now will help you with your future goals.**

I know kids as young as 11 or 12 years old who hold part-time jobs. They deliver newspapers, walk dogs and run errands. Ask your family, friends, neighbors and teachers for ideas that will pay you in both money and self-confidence.

Look for a job that interests you. If possible choose one which will help you reach a long-term goal. For example if you dream of becoming an architect, apply for work at a construction company or architectural firm.

Some Tips on Getting a Job:

☐ Choose a business you would like to work for and then make an appointment to meet the person in charge of hiring. Tell them of your interest and suggest ways you might be able to help them do their work (running errands, cleaning, making copies etc.). Often these jobs don't yet exist, but if you convince an employer you are reliable and self-motivated, they will be interested in hiring you.

☐ If you know the owner of the business or an employee who is in a position to put in a good word for you, making an appointment to talk with them about your interest will be helpful too.

☐ If you want to become a model someday, look for a part-time job as an assistant at a fitness club or a modeling school.

☐ Choosing a part-time job in this way will help you immensely when it comes time for you to choose a career. It will also allow you to begin to meet people in that field who can be valuable to you later on in life.

☐ If you can't find a part-time job that's related to an interesting career, look for work at the library, at your school or church or at a nearby restaurant or retail store. This kind of job will give you the opportunity of working with the public and you can use the experience to prepare yourself for later options.

☐ In the meantime however leave your job applications at places where you want to work. Then follow up with a telephone call every few weeks to see if they expect any openings.

☐ Business people are always looking for good workers who are reliable, trustworthy and self-motivated. Convince them you have these qualities and you'll get the job you want eventually.

If you have chores around the house, look at them as pre-job training and take pride in your accomplishments. You'll develop winning habits early.

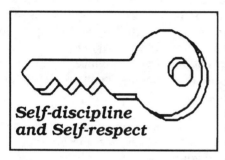

Self-discipline and Self-respect

Why do you need discipline and self-respect? When we're young we can do a lot for ourselves, but the best environment for growth and a good future is not to be unrestricted and totally free. The true freedom you crave is only possible when you achieve self-discipline and self-respect.

As much as you may not want me to say it, your parents can encourage your discipline by giving you responsibility and letting you earn their trust. If you're old enough for freedoms — e.g., staying out later, driving and/or buying a car, going out with friends, living alone, going off to college — then you'll be smart, responsible and earn your parent's respect — and your freedom.

Discipline means being firm and reasonable. Discipline means being efficient and effective. Discipline means getting the most out of your situation. Discipline means being a winner.

If your parents are smart, they'll encourage your willingness to accept new responsibilities, self-expression and freedom of thought. Now is the time for you to learn to spread your wings and fly.

Your parents should also accept you as you are and encourage you to accept yourself. Some people refer to this as self-love or self-respect. Whatever you call it the end result is the same: Winners are disciplined. Winners like themselves. They're able to recognize their limits but are also disciplined enough to go forward with their lives in a positive and constructive way.

Parental love and discipline go hand in hand and create your ability to love and discipline yourself.

If your first experiences with discipline were not provided by parents, you should have someone in your life to whom you can look for guidance: a guardian, an aunt or uncle, perhaps a grandparent or teacher. They should believe in using discipline with love as a tool to energize your reach for your goals.

Perhaps your experiences with discipline have been disappointing, particularly if someone demanded obedience from you. You may believe that the only way to cope is to rebel. I understand why you would feel that way. Unfortunately nothing could be further from the truth. You'll need a lot of self-discipline to grow up to be a winner in this kind of oppressive environment — but you can do it. First, put the past behind you. Then feel sorry for people who cannot live in a positive, healthy way. Finally look forward to your new future. You deserve only the best.

You may come from the inner city as I did. You may be living in a neighborhood which is mostly Italian, Irish, Jewish, Black or of some other ethnic origin. In this case your family may have values and practices that follow cultural lines.

You may be, or at least feel, restricted by these ethnic values. In that case remember: All cultures bring valuable perspectives on discipline that can enable you to live in harmony with other cultures and achieve your life goals.

If you are growing up in the kind of family spirit that for some reason is not what you believe to be disciplined and loving, you need to learn to love and discipline yourself. Look for someone to help you.

Don't let your fear of asking for help keep you from reaching for your dreams. Many of us have been where you are right now and we achieved our goals only because others have helped us along the way. Most of us want to give back to others that which has been given to us. All it takes is a question, "Can you take a few minutes to answer some of the questions I have about . . ."

Helpful Hints

- **Keep a list of your self-imposed rules in a visible place.**
- **Establish your own rewards for consistent, positive behavior.**
- **Make a list of planned action to take during the year.**
- **Set down your goals and a step-by-step plan of how to meet them.**
- **From time to time check your list and see how you're doing.**
- **Later, look back and see how you are progressing in life.**

If the first person you ask is not willing to help you, ask someone else. You'll be surprised to learn there are many people who are willing to help you.

Your ability to accept discipline in your life will be rewarded by self-respect — and respect from others.

It's this type of self-analysis, born of self-discipline, that's important. They're your goals, your plans and your checklist for personal progress. You're in charge. You do the grading.

Self-discipline and love of self are essential elements of winning.

You may have to look beyond your immediate family and friends to learn these skills but you can do it if you really want to be a winner.

No matter what the goal — winning in sports, success on the stock market, or reaching some personal victory — you are taking a risk to reach for it. Risk taking is part of winning.

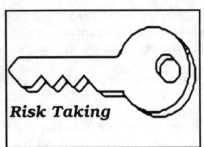

Risk Taking

Risk taking is a skill that can and should be learned. If you are fortunate you will learn within a supportive family setting. Some families allow children to participate in family decisions. In this instance, if you make an error in judgment or analysis, your parents will be able to help you. If you don't have this family support, you will have to use your own decision-making opportunities to learn successful risk taking.

Happy adolescents hold on to the asset of a protective home environment until they feel prepared to live on their own. Others are willing to take unnecessary risks such as moving away from home or using alcohol and drugs.

You must be convinced that the only risks that make sense offer a chance to win; drug and alcohol abuse offer only the certainty of failure. Even if your only goals are pleasure and excitement, drugs are not effective in reaching them, because drugs destroy confidence and self-respect.

Failure is part of taking risks but that DOES NOT mean that you're a failure.

If you fail, try to find out why and learn from the experience. Doing so is a sure sign of being a winner.

Learning to win means learning to fail. I am reminded of something told to me by a friend who was an avid cross-country skier. The first thing you learn about skiing, he said, is learning how to fall so you won't hurt yourself.

Learning to take risks is the same way. You will never get any-
where in life if you are not willing to take risks, but you need to know
that you may stumble on your journey to obtain your goals.

Since potential failure is an inevitable part of risk taking, respect for
failure must be learned early. Hurt and pain create strong feelings.
Exploring and respecting these feelings can help guide future actions.
Cover your bases before you take the risk, so you can see yourself as
a winner even if you don't reach a goal.

You are at the proper time in life to test all options and take positive
risks. When you get older, failing is harder to take and others expect
more from you.

Standing up to a battle is important for its own sake. The reason we
take risks is for the rewards. Even the most crushing disappointment
does not need to diminish the rewards of hard work, imagination, and
the learning experience. Instead of caving in to failure, you can come
through it stronger, more confident — and wiser.   These strengths
will help you reach for another goal.

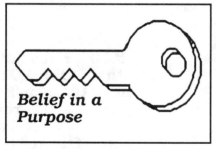

**Belief in a
Purpose**

Can a ship reach its destina-
tion without a charted course?
Can an architect build without
an idea of the purpose his crea-
tion will house? What is the
goal of a human life?

Many   generations   have
passed through this universe
without satisfactorily answer-
ing these questions. Yet you should ask yourself why you need to
reach for any goal beyond mere survival.

At some point we all come to realize the greatness of things, the
grandeur and the mystery of it all. We all have a purpose here. Un-

covering it, however, is sometimes a puzzle. To find your purpose, ask yourself, "Where do I, as one of the billions of people in this world, fit into this structure?" This type of question allows you to reflect on your purpose in life, your beliefs and your desires.

Your response to this question will not come to you overnight. But it will be of enormous assistance in determining what you want out of life, what your goals are going to be and how you are going to achieve those goals.

Some of us find no greater goal than serving others, or caring for the common good, e.g., working so that all human infants born on this planet have the opportunity to develop their inherent qualities to the fullest. Others of us believe our purpose should be to work to achieve a specific goal, or to help in the awakening of another person. What ever your purpose is here in this life — and everyone has one — never stop seeking until you find it. That purpose will serve to propel you out of even the lowest depths into the heights of achievement.

Your birth required timing and luck and these two components of winning will remain important throughout your life.

Timing and Luck

Of course, some of what you are is determined by the genes your parents gave you. Whether you are tall or short, whether your eyes are brown, blue or green, these decisions were made for you long ago.

The next roll of the dice comes with what your environment has to offer. Here the timing of your birth in history and the place of birth on the globe enter your chances for success. For example you could have been born in ancient Ethopia where the life expectancy for most children was only five years. Or you could have been born into a peasant's family during the 15th century. This would have allowed you little or no chance for making a better life for yourself — ever.

Luck and timing entered your life again by choosing the kind of parents you have, how much they love and care for you, the economic status of your family, your state of health, the quality of education you have access to, your neighborhood, friends and acquaintances. Many of these decisions have already been made for you and became important factors in determining who, what and where you are now.

No matter what "givens" you have to work with, no matter what foundation you have had laid for you, you have the ability to prepare today to become whatever you want to be. You need to develop your skills and abilities. You need to acquire knowledge. You need to work toward a healthy and satisfying goal. These are all elements you can choose without luck.

I knew a child who seems very lucky but who actually made her own luck. Mary grew up on a farm and was an "A" student in school. She wanted to go to college but went to a high school that did not offer chemistry. She read all of the books she could obtain on inorganic chemistry and took a chemistry exam that allowed her to enter college without having had a formal course in chemistry.

Mary had a goal, understood the requirements for attaining it and took the steps she was able to take to reach the goal. A losing attitude would have declared college entrance impossible, but Mary was a winner. She made herself lucky.

You can make your own luck with determination and a positive attitude.

Finally, faith is a crucial part of winning. It is the glue that holds together your hard work, your discipline, the risks you take, your belief in a purpose and your timing and luck. Never underestimate its effect on your future.

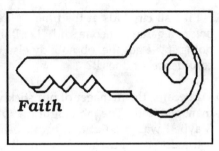

Faith

You may have faith in a higher power or some higher authority. You may have faith only in yourself and your fellow humans. Once you have it, you will begin to generate and exhibit a sense of personal power.

Faith provides ability, strength and courage when circumstances look most bleak. Energy springs from faith and grants you a peaceful perspective so that you can create new options, opportunities and change.

Faith allows you to dream, to dare, to act and to wait.

I believe that religion is that ready source of power and strength. I believe that if you have God's help, he has the odds on his side. Many important people and achievers agree with me. Many religious achievers use the term "we" to mean "the Lord and me."

Whatever your religious persuasion, whatever your beliefs, have faith in tomorrow, in yourself and in your ability to reach beyond your grasp.

Throughout life I have had to build my own self-confidence, and my own

Learning the Hard Way

winning attitude. But where did it come from? Is it something that comes about naturally? Looking back at my childhood, I have tried to find the moment I knew I had these skills.

Like all city kids at the time I played stickball in the street. Once before a game someone said, "Let Phil do the line-up, he doesn't mind doing it." I got the job nobody else wanted. This doesn't build self-confidence, or does it?

I became the manager of our stickball team not even knowing what managers did. The job taught me to evaluate the boys' hitting skills. Maybe I was good at that because I was not a good hitter myself. I learned to organize games with difficult and demanding kids. When we won, I felt good and confident. When we lost, I blamed myself.

This job of managing a ball team, the job no one else wanted, taught me valuable skills of leadership, organization and tenacity. Many years later these skills served me well as a managing physician of a clinic in Panama during World War II and as chairman of the Pediatrics Department at Georgetown University.

Does this story mean we need to be involved only in successful ventures to develop self-confidence? I think not.

What about failure? I had many failures. My mother wanted me to play the violin. Each hour of practice, I had one eye on the guys playing ball in the streets, the other watching for my mother. The music teacher knew I had no talent, but I guess he needed the quarters to stay alive in the Depression. I never became an accomplished violinist. I failed at the dream my mother had for me but it did not damage my self-esteem, because I did not seek this goal myself. Moreover, there was joy in my heart when I did not have to play that stupid fiddle anymore.

To this day I can't play a note. I never learned to read music.

Another failure did have consequences on my future — my performance in school. I was a poor student and had little or no encouragement in the classroom. This came back to haunt me when I wanted to apply to college. It was no consolation that I was the only student in my neighborhood to graduate. I was shocked by my letters of acceptance. I had been a failure in school — why did I even try?

I was able to overcome early obstacles and prior failures only because I was hungry to succeed. The desire to be a physician outweighed my low self-esteem.

Another obstacle to self-confidence I faced was my physical appearance. I developed severe acne at 16. My mother dismissed it saying, "It's a stage you are going through." But I was miserable and desperate.

I remember wondering why this had to happen to me. I felt unwanted and ugly through several years of college. But in a way these feelings made me develop other social skills. I became a good dancer and also a clown to make people laugh during those trying adolescent years.

The reason I am telling you these memories is so that you will know that the trials you may be going through are part of growing up. I know that is no consolation to you. But I also know that you can achieve your goals if you just take it a day at a time and try to do your best each day. With every day that goes by you will be more and more a winner.

Summary

☐ A winner's attitude is honed by hard work, discipline, risk taking, strong belief in a purpose, faith and proper timing or luck. It must be backed by self-discipline and self-respect.

☐ Be prepared to take risks and to profit from the experience of failing.

☐ Learn to examine what happened if you did not succeed and draw up a new game plan to avoid repeating the same mistakes.

☐ Take an overview of your goals and then work toward them day-by day, knowing you can win in the long run.

Note To Parents, Teachers and Counselors:

We need to help to-day's youth learn that the work ethic is alive and well. A child of 11 or 12 can hold a part-time job. But most young people, even older teens, need help finding work. About 75 percent of the jobs young people hold came through introductions made by a family member, friends or a civic-minded person. The time spent using your imagination and contacts to help a young person gain a job is one of the best investments you can make. They need a lot of encouragement to seek employment and land a job. They need praise for tackling the project and for work well done. Give them a hand, both in assisting in finding work and applause when they do. Learning the incentive to work early will help keep them headed in the right direction later.

Adults can forget that older children need nuturing, too; it just assumes a more mature, subtle form. Teens need their belief in themselves nurtured, their constructive plans encouraged. Let's put nurturing young people's talents and dreams back in the home and classrooms. Criticism can be constructive if balanced with praise. But constant criticism or indifference can be a real "downer." We all seek approval of some sort. If youth get it from positive role models, they aren't as likely to seek out approval from poor (destructive) peer groups. Those who are the most difficult to deal with probably need nurturing the most.

Chapter 2

Motivate Yourself: Your Seven Steps

What is motivation? At the biological level, your body is well equipped to provide for its own survival needs. Experiments have shown, however, that with motivation it is possible to overcome even the instinct to survive. What a powerful process!

Each one of us can harness this energy to overcome anger, frustration and pain in our lives. As a young adult, you may feel you are trapped by one or more of the many overwhelming problems which tend to creep into our lives as we grow up.

> **Harness your energy and focus it toward success**

You may have to live in an unhappy family; you may feel you are all alone and that no one cares about you. You may be feeling the intense pressures of what I call "the good-life game" from your parents and teachers: Making at least a 3.5, going to the "right" college, naming "the" career which will assure you a good future. Or you may be on drugs or alcohol; you may live in a ghetto.

You may feel there is no way out. I'm here to tell you how to use this tool, motivation, to help you get out and get going.

1 Step Away From The Chaos

The first step is to bring some calm out of any chaos you may be feeling. Don't expect too much from yourself. Some of the decisions that you have to make under the age of 25 can be all-consuming. So don't worry if you feel confused. I know many adults who would be unable to make good decisions of the kind you are having to make.

Adults sometimes forget that young adults are expected to make decisions that affect the rest of their lives — without experience on which to base their decisions. No wonder many of our young people seek escape from the problems around them.

2 Focus On Your Goal

The second step is to focus on what you want out of life. Begin to link your dreams with planning for adulthood and employment.

Focusing on a goal can be difficult if you are a teenager who is actively engaged in school activities, friendships, social functions, a part-time job, meeting family needs — or watching television.

3 Accept Your Goal

The third step is goal acceptance. Yes, you must choose goals in life which are compatible with your dreams and your talents and you should start choosing activities that will ultimately advance the goal.

It is important for you to remember that your goals, your career choices, your campus selections are not set in concrete. During this time of your life your decisions should be considered flexible.

A fourth step in this process is to gather information about the goal.

4 Gather Information

- Who do you know who can help you find information about your goal?

- What does achievement of your goal require in time, money and commitment?

- Where can you find the resources to achieve your goal?

- What kind of talents and skills do you have which will aid you in achieving your goal?

- What is the likelihood of achieving success?

The fifth step is reflection. Reaching beyond your grasp is filled with a sense of uncertainty and possibly fear.

5 Reflect On What You Want

This is a time to reflect on what you are. What do you see yourself as, in adult life? Do you see yourself as you are, in the same cultural environment, only older, or do you see something different, someone who has achieved more than your present status or even greater than your own parents and family?

Perhaps you have a more mature concept of self, a desire to support others and help in the community. Which will it be? Should you dare to dream, then the risk is worth taking.

Obviously this process is a most difficult one, especially if you should have many demands made upon you by your friends, family and teachers.

For example, if you live in the inner city or a ghetto you may have poweful forces striving to keep you there. In that case you are risking failure to get out. You may feel terribly confused when those close to you are negative about your plans for the future.

If you are a socially advantaged youth, you may feel the need to reject your parents' affluence. Again you may feel confused, become negative and develop a loser's attitude.

A Positive Attitude Helps

Don't fall into the loser's trap. A loser sees only the dark end of things. He or she is cynical about life, family and people in general. A loser is afraid and masks fear with cynicism.

If you are caught in this trap, there is only one way out: positive thinking. You can reach for your dreams. It is a risk but you can do it and if you keep trying, eventually you will make it.

The best time for you to successfully begin to reach beyond your grasp is 15 to 18 years of age. For example, if you want to enter the professional fields of engineering, science, medicine, physics, a strong effort is needed in high school.

It is interesting to note here that in the United States fewer people are choosing science and engineering as careers. Experts predict that those fields will be short some half-million people by the 21st century.

These kinds of predictions about the future can help you make choices today. Talk to your teachers and others who know about the career you're considering; research your subject before you make a decision.

The sixth step in this process is the expectation of success. Research shows that people who expect success actually achieve it more often than those who don't.

6 **Expect Success**

Expect success even if you do not consider yourself a "natural" winner. You may have failed to reach your goals in the past; you may have a physical disability; maybe you are clumsy or hyperactive. All these things can be overcome.

Schools pay more attention to learning disabilities than ever before, but they are not infallible. If you are having difficulty, talk to one of your teachers, a school counselor, or a doctor. Support services are available to help you understand your problem and succeed in spite of it.

The seventh and last step: live with your dream. Have someone in your life who believes in you and will encourage you when you're discouraged or tired and just don't think you can go on.

7 **Live With Your Dreams**

When I was growing up, I had my mother to inspire me to things greater than I even knew. She was always saying things that planted the seeds in my mind about being a doctor: "You know, my son said 'I want to be a doctor when I grow up.' What a wonderful thing to be a doctor. My son, the doctor." My magnificent mother embarrassed me no end with this story. But there is no question in my mind that she was the driving force in my ambition to become a physician.

Probably in no other period in our history have young people had so many opportunities for future success. In the 19th century the Industrial Revolution brought great opportunities but it also brought mass exploitation of children in poverty and need.

The Depression of the 1930s gave a generation of youth the will and the fight to survive and win but it was a time of great deprivation. The 1960s saw doubt, dissent and despair even about American values.

In the 1970s, the United States made progress in consumer protection and environmental awareness but was shaken by the Iran hostage crisis — a great nation made captive by a small country once our ally. We also lost the competitive edge in the marketplace to foreign nations.

Now, once again, we are involved in a crisis in the Middle East which challenges our position as the world-wide protector of freedom, our ranking in world power, the well-being of the human race and the stability of the global economy. Our youth in the military must exercise utmost self-discipline and be motivated by a winning attitude as they face a most difficult situation.

In spite of the world situation the 1990s offer exciting possibilities in new technologies and great challenges in a rapidly transforming world economy. The next century belongs to you, if you can meet its challenges.

Summary

☐   You can fire yourself up and get going with motivation.

☐   Choose a path and learn to focus on your dreams and plans.

☐   Choose activities and develop talents that will carry you forward to your goal.

☐   Learn to screen out distractions and non-productive activities.

☐   Be realistic about your goal and take it step-by-step. If you are sure of what you want, don't let others distract from your ambitions.

☐   Expect to succeed and associate with someone who will give you encouragement and inspiration.

☐   Remember: Reach beyond your grasp, work hard, examine all options and go for it!

Note To Parents, Teachers and Counselors:

An Eight-Point Plan to Help Children Succeed

Young people today need time to reflect on their goals and the action they need to take to achieve their goals. Waiting until kids are in high school to focus on careers may be too late. By then a student may have wasted important academic opportunities. A 10-year-old is mature enough to begin thinking about what to do with his or her life.

If we truly want our children to succeed and our country to have a sound future, we must fulfill our own obligations to them. We, too, must reach beyond mediocrity and complacency.

1. We must expect the best from ourselves as a nation. We cannot quietly relinquish our former economic greatness because we now have other competitors in the world's markets. If we readily accept losing, what can we expect from the next generation?

2. We must build a great education system. Like Japan we must respect teachers, pay them well and give them time to learn and teach. We must also improve our ability to recognize the individual's potential. Not everyone can excel in the academic curriculum, but we can direct students into areas where they can succeed without feeling like second-class citizens.

3. We must look for ways to support the large number of single parents. Nobody can do it alone — we have to be creative in finding supports for these disadvantaged families.

4. We must redouble our efforts to rid the schools and streets of drugs. More drug education in the schools and at home will help but what is needed is a direct strategic approach to support the environment in which our children are growing.

5. We need programs for our young future mothers so they may deliver healthy babies. Child care and parenting should be a top priority for our country as a nation. At the same time, programs teaching the enormous responsibilities of parenthood need to be increased to help reduce the high number of unwed teenage mothers.

6. Employable skills must be taught to all young people and drop-out prevention programs should be instituted in all schools.

7. Dignity should be restored to the families who fall into the lower 25 percent of the national income. Adequate, clean and safe housing is a must here.

8. Local education centers should be established depending upon the need, the location and the resources required. Programs could be based in schools, hospitals, churches etc. The focus should be multidisciplinary such as health, road work, housing, transportation, whatever.

Chapter 3

Choose Your Own Role Models

We've all heard the term "role model." You may think of a famous athlete, an actor or actress or some other public figure as your role model. Actually, however, your most important role model is someone you know and admire, someone with whom you feel comfortable.

For many of us our first role models are our parents. We usually resemble our parents and we love them. It is hard to see ourselves as very different from them.

We feel only shame and embarrassment if our parents do things of which we're not proud. I know many kids who live with the frequent nightmare of a father who is arrested for selling drugs or a mother who gets drunk.

If you have poor role models for parents or guardians you may lack a good self-image. Even though you're not to blame for your parents' behavior, you feel a sense of disrespect, for your parents and for yourself.

Do You Have Poor Role Models?

Your progress into adulthood may be much more difficult if you are growing up in a one-parent family, or one that is culturally apart from the rest of society. While you are going through a period of rapid change physically, psychologically and sexually — and trying to deal with all those new feelings — you may feel you have no support. You may feel that you are alone.

Turn Fear Into Challenge	You can use this as a challenge to grow up quickly. Many of our greatest entertainers, business people and politicians propelled themselves out of terrible home environments to become successful. Many of them used the market place and the street as testing grounds for their adult life rather than a more conventional schoolroom and campus.

When you accept these challenges and use your own abilities to bring yourself up to a productive, responsible life, you stand a good chance of successfully making the transition from adolescent to adult. A role model can be a source of great strength and motivation.

What To Look For In A Role Model

Even if your family is supportive and loving you will want a role model — or mentor — as you grow up. This will help you keep that focus we talked about in Chapter 2.

If you fail to find an effective role model early in life then often your peer group becomes your behavioral pacesetter. The consequences of this can be disastrous. If you want to succeed, you must look beyond your peers for help and inspiration.

⇨ Characteristics

The first step is to find someone who can act as a role model for you. Characteristics of a good role model include:

- ☐ Someone you can count on to be there for you

- ☐ Someone you identify as the type of person you wish to be

- ☐ An industrious person

- ☐ An established person of good character

- ☐ Someone who has a reasonable record of successful accomplishments

- ☐ A sensitive and sharing person

- ☐ You must have a sense that you both share similar values, perhaps come from like backgrounds or have a common understanding about life.

⇨ Time To Spend With You

Secondly, the good role model you seek isn't just a person to imitate. Rather, the person must be able to take the time to help you work through your problems, make recommendations and help you find successful solutions.

⇨ Helpful

Third, the role model should be able to help you to learn to think things through for yourself.

Summary

☐   We all need someone to look up to; someone who can show us how to "handle it." Often we must go outside the family to find a role model, or to fortify family role models.

☐   Find someone you trust whom you look up to and who cares about your development. Work with them so you learn to trust your own reasoning. It may be hard to find such a person, but don't give up the search.

☐   Learn to respect the knowledge your elders have gained though experience. Within your own peer group, pick your peers carefully.

☐   Join groups that provide positive experiences.

Note To Parents, Teachers and Counselors:

Obviously if prior identification of a good role model cannot be experienced in the home or community, the school setting could provide a controlled atmosphere in which to test it. The need is to develop in youth the ability to examine options and successfully choose the most productive outcome, ultimately setting a pattern for a winning behavior.

Many students who achieve success in adulthood frequently remember a person, usually a teacher, a member of the clergy, a family member, someone who cared enough to relate and share.

It's been noted that youth place special values on activities exhibited by desirable models. Remember, however, whoever determines the nature of desirable models will ultimately have this decision tested in society.

Society at large, then, is an effective force in this decision. When youths are without a roof over their heads, clothes on their backs or food in their stomachs it becomes very difficult to define desirability in role models. Yet, and foremost, adult society will punish for behavior not in keeping with the established norms.

Predictions of how youth responds to contradictory practices within our society are difficult, yet repetitious success in role model identification does allow for a pattern of adoption of a role model.

Success must be identified by the youths themselves, only they can make this judgment. The end result is dependent on the cultural designators of desirability as related to honesty, integrity, strength, with learning and intelligence. Once this process is complete and they have attained self-respect they are prepared to test their concepts in society. At first it may be mastering as simple a tool as a skateboard. It obviously becomes important then to compete with others in skateboard activities.

Youth must understand early that the rules by which the game of life is played must be fair to all. Should one risk breaking the rules, in the long run, such behavior will be defeating and prevent long term gains.

This process of playing within the rules and attaining success is easily understood. Suppose, however, that one continues to play by the rules but does not achieve "success" as defined by him, then what? Re-evaluate the goals, resources, motivation and energy level to reach the desired success. Long-term goals and accomplishments demand greater dedication, work and discipline than short-term goals. Usually, however, a set of more easily accomplished objectives added to a long term accomplishment does have merit.

To give clear examples of such an experience, a boy born in a low socio-economic environment is desirous of becoming a scientist or a physician. This goal requires awareness of long years of commitment to education, approximately 25 percent of his life span, financial burdens totaling more than the family can earn in a decade. If the youth is in an inappropriately structured family environment, he must gain outside financial support. Almost impossible? But probable with the right mix.

The early necessary ingredient is a true desire to achieve a long-term goal. Usually this is initiated in the early school grades 5 to 8. This desire at first may be unrealistic but a perceived goal, a noble goal does give some credence to the character of the youth. But without encouragement and planning, choosing a goal can be meaningless. A higher education is needed to reach such high goals.

Right now in this country the drop-out rate in school is incredibly high, between 30 to 50 percent. The first milestone of success for a young person is to finish school and earn an opportunity to enter college. Getting over this hurdle is not easy but it can be done if the youth has the desire to reach high, work hard and identify with the proper role model.

Chapter 4

Be Creative!

What does creativity have to do with reaching beyond your grasp? Why is it important to you?

Many have tried to define creativity. The essence of it, however, is original, inven-

First, Let's Define the Word

tive, ingenious, imaginative and valuable production which results from the focus of the brain committed to the power to invent.

The reason this is important to you is you are living in a dynamic and exciting time. During your lifetime, you will see many changes and technological advances. You need to be able to successfully adapt. This requires your ability to be creative.

Think about it. Our planet is over 4 billion years old. Over 10,000 years ago, humans began to reason and express themselves. Just over

A Look Back

2,000 years ago the Greeks applied numbers and logic together to create a discipline which today has branched into computer technology, performing high-speed mathematics and solving complex problems with ease.

But it has only been in the last two centuries that people have made such enormous strides, joining theory and scientific discovery, to shape life as we know it today.

Consider Your Potential
Role in the Following Fields

⇨ Physics

Using mathematics to explain the basic laws of the natural sciences of mass and energy movement, physics exploded when Albert Einstein described the relationship of mass and energy as being forms of each other, i.e., the theory of relativity. Physics has developed theories of fundamental forces such as electromagnetism, nuclear force and gravity.

You can be involved in the excitement that is forthcoming in this field. It is because of many people like you that we have progressed from thinking of the atom as simply a nice structure with some functioning parts to the realization that it is one of the most complex particles of energy to be found and harnessed.

⇨ Chemistry

The study of substances and their changing forms was first noted by the Egyptians who mixed metals at boiling points to create new substances, e.g., bronze. This discipline finally emerged to produce organic compounds which later were synthetically produced to give us the large field of polymerization, i.e., plastics. Creativity has progressed in quantum leaps during the past few centuries.

⇨ Astronomy

The stars, of course, were always with even the most ancient of societies, tracing the seasons and lighting their paths at night by land and sea. But it was not that long ago when the Greeks created a discipline to study the structure and function of the universe.

More recently, exploration of outer space has added to our knowledge, particularly with theories regarding origin of satellites and planets. And the Hubble telescope was launched toward outer space in 1990 in our attempt to look back in time.

Now you have the opportunity of asking questions such as, "What is a black hole and how does this come about? Is the universe expanding or contracting?" The list of adventures ready for you in space is as endless as the skies above.

⇨ Health

It was not that long ago when physicians were attaching leeches to their patients in an effort to cure a variety of illness. Only in this century has our life expectancy dramatically increased. Now organ replacements, genetics and knowledge about DNA structure (deoxyribonucleic acid) not only extend a human life but enhance it. This is a fascinating field of study.

We have conquered many illnesses, such as tuberculosis, syphilis, pneumonia, meningitis, only to find new outbreaks and new immune strains. Challenges are ever-present in the medical profession.

You could be the next scientist to unravel the mystery about cancer or AIDS (Acquired Immune Deficiency Syndrome).

⇨ Engineering

Engineering science and technology have produced many astonishing accomplishments in the last 150 years.

- ☐ The Eiffel Tower built in the latter part of the 19th century.
- ☐ Alexander Bell invented the telephone in 1876.
- ☐ Roentgen discovered the x-ray in 1895.
- ☐ Thomas Edison invented the electric incandescent light in 1879.
- ☐ The first successful flight in a motor-driven plane, credited to Orville and Wilbur Wright, took place in 1903.
- ☐ The mass-production of automobiles didn't start until Henry Ford opened his Model T assembly line in 1913.

You have incredible opportunities available to you in this field if you can light the spark in that part of your brain called the creativity center.

⇨ Social Behavior

The art of one society living in harmony with other societies will require new tools to study this discipline. Today many aspects of our society are weak.

These fields of study are hardly a century old, and yet their importance is paramount.

Family structure in the United States is changing. What used to be considered the unit of society's structure — the family of two parents and children, with grandparents close by for added support — is changing. More than 20 million one-parent families or fractured families now make up our society.

The science of human behavior is an exciting field and deserves and will receive dedicated effort on the part of many of your peers.

Soon the world will have a population of 6 billion; we must learn to live in harmony. The fields of psychology, cultural anthropology and the social sciences will be arenas where contributions will be meaningful.

➪ Education

How can we challenge the young minds in our country and all over the world? The answers to formal education and drop-outs must be forthcoming. Why is it that some human beings continue to learn throughout life and others don't?

Challenges facing education professionals have never been greater. You could be on the cutting edge of helping to bring the U.S. educational system to the forefront in the future. Our society is only as strong as is our educational system.

➪ Economics

A field pertaining to finance, economics is another area deserving a new global approach. Critics say that U.S. economists focus only upon abstract models and shed little light on the practical applications of economics.

The behavior of economic laws needs to be equated with people's actions. Society as well as the individual clearly has rights and privileges that haven't yet been successfully addressed by economists.

This is a challenge you could tackle. We need bright young creative minds like yours to help confront the problems of the changing economies around the world.

➪ The Arts

People who choose the arts — music, visual arts, literature — for a career often have a God-given talent. In a way, it's as though they've been chosen to do that job. You may have this kind of talent. But no matter how talented you are, it will still take motivation and hard work to succeed.

In exploring and developing your abilities, you may find you are best at combining creative talent with intellectual pursuits. It's a powerful combination.

Consider Renaissance artist, Leonardo da Vinci. The whole world recognizes his portrait of the *Mona Lisa*. Yet, da Vinci didn't feel that painting alone accomplished his goals. He worked as an engineer and an architect, and studied anatomy, botany and other sciences. He believed his scientific productivity surpassed his artistic works.

Da Vinci's famous drawing of the human figure in a circle, which showed that a man's reach equaled his height, demonstrates the successful pairing of artistic talent and scientific discovery.

Many great people have overcome seemingly impossible circumstances to succeed.

One example of a great artist whose life was a well-documented struggle is Michelangelo. His mother died when he was six. His father was mean, vain and indifferent. Michelangelo didn't start school until he was 10.

This doesn't sound like a very good start for a young boy, yet he is considered one of the geniuses of the Renaissance. His masterpieces include: the Dome of St. Peter's in Rome; frescoes in the Sistine Chapel; the sculptures *Pieta* and *David*.

The genius of an artist often isn't recognized until after death, but

Arthur Schlesinger, Jr., a noted historian and author, observed qualities needed to nurture the creative process: "Observation, reflection, imagination, invention and judgment." This creative process is not limited to the arts.

Many young people overlook scientific research as being a "creative" process. But once bitten by the research bug, it is difficult for many to consider any other work.

The same sense of accomplishment is felt when a newspaper reporter sees his or her story in print, with his or her name in the byline. The excitement of meeting deadlines, covering top stories and receiving pay for work well done keeps the creative juices flowing.

You need to find the field that will allow you to achieve success using your creative abilities. Finding the right place will be a challenge. Enjoy it! Whether it be in the arts, sciences or any other field, you have a rightful place in society.

Michelangelo received much acclaim for his work during his lifetime. Even so, life wasn't easy for him. Local politics interfered with his work and he was often short of money. Once he spent a year creating a bronze sculpture for Pope Julius II, only to have it melted down for battle armaments as soon as it was finished.

In spite of his fame, Michelangelo was never satisfied with what he created. At the height of his popularity, he proclaimed, "Painting and sculpture have ruined me. It would have been better if in my youth I had hired myself out to make sulfur matches."

Michelangelo was a talented genius, but he was successful because he worked hard and was never quite satisfied with his accomplishments. He dared to dream, to reach beyond his grasp.

A Woman's Place is in the. . .

Every day more women are accepting the challenges of business, science, education, the arts, and combining career and family. Although we've made progress in eliminating sexist attitudes and establishing equal opportunity and pay, more is needed. Today's world does not come close to true equality.

Women have developed many skills over the generations: a keen sensitivity and understanding of human behavior; family-oriented and nurturing; and, because of the duality of roles that women must assume, many women have developed excellent organizational and management skills.

Young women can use these abilities as cornerstones for developing a career and becoming more assertive in the boardrooms across America.

The United States can and will catch up with per capita productivity when the marketplace allows for both sexes to achieve to their full capacity. Creativity shall then take on another dimension.

Summary

☐ It will take great creativity to resolve the problems and challenges of the 21st century. There are exciting opportunities ahead in all fields for those who reach out for them and are not afraid to try new approaches.

☐ Young women need to use to greater advantage their natural instincts for organizing and managing to make headway in the professional world.

☐ The future belongs to you. All you have to do is reach for it, question it and become excited enough to be the next Einstein, the next Henry Ford, the next Alexander Graham Bell. Your part of this ageless growth of the universe is waiting for you right outside your door.

☐ Your creative ability can and will play a crucial role in the successes gained the next century.

Note To Parents, Teachers and Counselors:

Creativity is needed to solve the problems facing society today. It must be fostered; the gains and rewards will reach far beyond the Nobel Laureate.

A successful challenge to the creativity of our young people is only possible in a positive environment. You — through our educational system, through individual sponsorship and through corporate involvement — can help our young people focus on achievement.

The Educational System: Teachers need to be paid salaries commensurate with their responsibility. They hold the key to the future of this great nation and that of civilization. The only valid education stimulates the creativity and imagination of our most important asset: our children.

Receptive Adults: In order for our children to command creative challenge and pursue excellence, those in the home must be receptive to a child's struggle to achieve.

Intimidation by criticism is not only immature but destructive. Adults must help youth learn to view challenge as an adventure into uncharted waters. They need to develop critical insight. Positive results and healthy feedback will help establish a good self-image.

The family lays this foundation for a child's future success.

• Sponsorship: An additional factor affecting the creativity of our children is a receptive audience on the part of the community. Sponsorship is obtainable and affordable, as many scientists, artists, diplomats and theologians, can attest. In recent years, individual patrons have donated billions of dollars to philanthropic foundations

tions for sponsorship of creative minds. The U. S. Congress and executive branch of our government also provide funding for those with exceptional talent.

The Marketplace: Nine out of ten of the largest banks in the world are Japanese. Private and corporate debt in this country is $8 trillion. Foreign production of electronics, cars and steel has crippled America's industry. The United States has begun to get fat; it must learn once again to keep pace with change.

Many of the brightest minds in the country go into law, the stock market, and corporate consulting firms. But new and more creative approaches are needed in other segments of the marketplace as the United States struggles to keep its place in this fast-paced, global economy.

Is there a market for creativity? There should be. Corporate America needs to reach out and touch today's young people. Through involvement in the educational system, corporate sponsorships and individual mentoring, our young people can be inspired to help our country remain a world leader.

Chapter 5

Communication

"Why," you may think, "is communication important for success? I can read and write. What else is necessary?"

Most conversations are methodical exchanges of information. True communication requires much more. To be an effective communicator, you must accept responsibility not only for delivery of the message but also for its acceptance.

We must recognize our dependence on the culture of our birth. Like it or not, we reflect our family, race, and nationality. I empathize with those who live in this country but cannot think, speak and listen in English. The trauma left me with a temporary stutter and lack of self-esteem.

The spoken word is crucial, but not the only means of communication. We communicate our ideas and values through every facet of our lives: art, architecture, music and dance, law, government, engineering and religion.

Just because we open our mouths and talk to someone doesn't mean we are communicating with them.

I learned about the importance of good communication very early in life. A touchy male teacher in primary school had declared the punishment for not doing homework was to copy the *Constitution of the United States*, 100 times by the following day.

Learn To Communicate Clearly. Otherwise what you say and what the other person hears could be two different things.

I raised my hand and asked, "Suppose we don't want to do that?"

The teacher went into a rage and threw his book at me. (My desk was in the back of the class, so I wasn't badly hurt.) What I had meant to say was, "Is there an alternative to that particular punishment?"

As a direct result of my inability to clearly communicate, I was labeled a tough guy by my peers, and it became difficult for me to volunteer in class. Communication had broken down. To this day, I vividly remember parts of the *Constitution*.

The ancient Greeks communicated profound ideas in their theaters, using costumes, settings, lighting, masks, music and the spoken word. The Romans used engineering to bind the Roman Empire together with aquaducts and roads. World religions have united people with common beliefs. Law and government codify a country's moral and ethical concepts.

Without ignoring the importance of the wide realm of human communication, you must be able to speak effectively with other people. School achievement and job success depend on good verbal communication skills.

Responsibility For The Delivery

To a great extent, the responsibility for what your audience — whether it be one person or a group — hears is yours. Sometimes "people hear what they want to hear;" but if you're an effective speaker, you'll be able to control your audience's reaction.

To be a good communicator, you must be a good observer. If your audience looks bored, if they fidget and yawn, you may not be getting your message across. If they frown or smile at inappropriate times, they may be getting the wrong message.

You can't assume your audience speaks your language. Using slang terms and words that are "in" with your peer group may sound like a foreign language to a prospective employer. Be sure you find a common ground for communication.

As you speak, observe the reaction of your audience. Doing so will tell you if your message is being received correctly.

Writing can be a more exact form of communication than conversation or a speech, although you might think it is easier to explain yourself in a conversation than in writing.

No matter what career you choose, you will probably need both verbal and written skills. Not everyone needs to speak like Jesse Jackson or write like Tom Wolfe, but successful leaders, business and professional people have to get their message across.

Some Tips for Good Communication

☐ Know your subject. Use concrete examples and specifics.

☐ Know your audience.

☐ Be concise and make your position, perspective, or limitations clear.

☐ Avoid repetition of non-essential facts or catchwords.

☐ Pay attention to the response you receive.

☐ Avoid arguments.

☐ Be flexible and modify your delivery or language if it is not being received.

☐ If you're speaking to a group, strengthen your verbal message with pictures, sound and other aids.

☐ Be aware of the messages you send with body language and your appearance.

☐ In written communication looks count too. Make your letter or proposal as attractive as possible. Pay special attention to neatness.

Responsibility of the Receiver

How many times have you accused your parents — or some other adult — of not listening to you? Many times what you're really saying is that you weren't able to make them see your point of view.

When you learn to be a better communicator, you'll be able to improve your success on that score. But to really solve the problem, you need their cooperation, too. The listener — your audience — has to be willing to communicate. Being open-minded is a must.

How often have you listened to your parents, with your mind already made up, unwilling to see things their way? Put yourself in their place and you'll see what you both are up against. Recognizing the problem is the first step toward solving it.

You've heard it before, but communication is definitely a two-way street.

As a listener, you have a responsibility to know the difference between fact and hype. We're bombarded all the time with products labeled "new." We often assume that means improved or better. It's a hype.

Being an open-minded listener doesn't mean believing everything you hear. Communication is not complete until your questions have been answered. You have a responsibility to find out the facts behind the hype.

? **Listen to others — you may learn something but don't be afraid to question what you hear.**

A 30-second news flash on television recently showed a reporter saying, "There is a question regarding defective parts on air equipment purchased by the government. The firm says it checked into the defective parts and found none."

The reporter then added, "If indeed defective parts were delivered, then the taxpayers were indeed cheated."

You as the listener need to question the intent of that story. Were taxpayers cheated? They weren't, so what was the news? It sounds as though the reporter didn't want to be "cheated" out of a story that might have been sensational if it had been true.

It's the same as saying, "If you had shot me, I'd be dead. But you didn't and I'm not." There is no story but the implication is that a crime was intended. Many people, if they didn't listen carefully, might assume a crime was committed.

Freedom of speech and freedom of the press are basic rights that Americans cherish. But with those rights come responsibilities. If misinterpretation — poor communication — is a problem for professional communicators on national television, you can bet it's an even bigger problem for all the rest of us. We as listeners must help guard against misinterpretation by questioning the hype and understanding the facts.

Summary

☐   If you have one of the greatest ideas in the world, it will do no good unless you can communicate it effectively to others.

☐   You have a responsibility to deliver your message clearly and to see that it is received and interpreted properly.

☐   As a listener you have a responsibility to keep an open mind and make sure you have the facts before you consider the communication complete.

☐   Developing good communication skills requires understanding your subject and your audience. These skills are signs of maturity and you'll find them useful in all areas of your life.

☐   Today we are bombarded with information, from junk mail to 30-second news flashes on television. You need to be informed well enough on important issues to be able to discriminate between factual accounts and misinforming hype.

☐   Make sure when you communicate with people that you're giving them the facts, not just the hype.

☐   Observe successful communicators — your favorite teachers, for example, or a religious leader who keep your attention. Read. These are two ways to develop your own communication skills.

Note to Parents, Teachers and Counselors:

Communication, beyond the most basic forms, is unique to human beings. We've entered an era of high-speed, high-tech global communications. But all the computers and FAX machines in the world won't replace our need to speak or write — and listen — effectively.

Encouraging young people to read, to analyze what they are reading, hearing and seeing will help them be better informed and better communicators themselves.

Adults also need to set good examples and need to listen to young people. Usually the "generation gap" is nothing more than a communication gap.

There should be more emphasis on effective communication in the home, school and even social settings. Let young people take active roles in educational skits and debates. It gives them good practice and insight into the complexity of "simple" or basic communications. Writing exercises help them refine these skills.

Introduction To
Chapters 6, 7, 8

Setting Limits

What's happening to our society? Short-term goals supercede long-range ideals. The "Now Generation" wants instant gratification, rewards up front, here and now; fame and fortune are dished up like fast foods.

"What's in it for me?" echoes from the school room to the executive suite. Where's the sense of responsibilty individuals should have for our society, our civilization?

Athletics, a basic training ground for individual and team achievement, seems to be focused on sprinting to the top. Our long-term race for survival has been ignored.

Athletes cheat by taking steroids to improve their performance for the next competition without a care for future implications. Some get "hyped" for a game by using illegal drugs, an action which could destroy their bodies and their careers.

The "Now" crowd contends: Everybody does it; everybody cheats and those who don't will be left out in the cold. When you're hot, you're hot. When you're not, you're not.

Innocent babies contract a deadly disease called AIDS because of their parents' unwise sexual habits.

Those who indulge in un-safe sex are still saying, "If it feels good, do it."

No one wants to feel unduly restricted or limited. But there's a big difference between making the most of unlimited opportunities and jumping on a bandwagon bound for destruction without asking the price of the ticket.

What in the world happened to restricting one's behavior for one's own good and for the good of society and humankind? Where's a little common sense self-restraint?

Let's look at some cold hard facts. Perhaps better knowledge about the side effects from steroids, the ravages of drug abuse and sexual promiscuity will put the cost of **not** setting limits in perspective.

Chapter 6

Setting Limits on Steroid Use

The use of anabolic steroids was banned by the International Olympic Committee in 1976. Competitors who use steroids are subject to severe sanctions. Ben Johnson, a Canadian sprinter, won an Olympic Gold Medal in 1988 and had it taken away three days later because tests showed he had used anabolic steroids.

Anabolic steroids are illegal unless prescribed by a doctor.

Studies have been done to prove that anabolic steroids improve athletic performance. The results have been mixed, but no double-blind study has ever been able to prove that assumption. Consequently scientists, doctors and athletic professionals don't agree on the value of steroid use.

Even so, steroids are still widely used. A recent study among male high school seniors showed the usage rate on a school-wide basis to be 68.7 percent.

Twenty-one percent of steroid users reported the primary source of the drug was a health professional. Coaches and gym attendants were identified as the suppliers by 20 percent of the students.

The use of steroids has been linked to heart attacks, strokes, liver disease, cancer, sterility and psychosis. Reports have surfaced of deaths related to long-term use of high doses of anabolic steroids.

Anabolic steroids are derivatives of testosterone, the male sexual hormone. Testosterone promotes masculine characteristics, even in females. Anabolic steroids have been formulated to produce muscular growth and increase strength without the masculinizing effects.

On the surface, this sounds promising. It's not so simple, however, to separate the growth functions from the masculinizing ones. Athletes using anabolic steroids risk incurring both hormone functions.

During adolescence, the body increases testosterone to promote masculinity in the male. In the female it interacts with the sex hormone estrogen. Obvious signs of biological sexual maturity and physical growth take place, changing boys into young men and girls into young women.

Before you begin to tinker with Mother Nature, think about the possible consequences. Don't be naive and think that you can artificially change the structure of your sexuality and not suffer side effects.

Using steroids or any other kind of drug may plant a ticking time bomb in your body.

It's a complex process and can be disturbed by the administration of steroids for athletic purposes. Taking steroids can affect the body's cells, genes and hormones.

Aside from the medical complications listed, side effects can include: male breast enlargement; increased acne; and water retention.

The effects of anabolic steroids are not only physical. In a study of 41 subjects in Massachusetts and Los Angeles, five developed psychotic symptoms when they took steroids. When they stopped taking the drug, the symptoms went away.

Steroids can also cause depression, manic anxieties and even a panic disorder.

Be smart. Don't risk physical and mental harm — don't risk AIDS — when it's not even been proved that steroids can make you a better athlete.

Bigger doesn't always mean better. Don't be willing to blindly try any quick fix to win.

Reaching beyond your grasp means playing fair and winning by the rules. If you cheat and change the rules to suit yourself, you're no longer in the same game. You can't be a true winner.

Another side effect is beginning to show up from steroid use. Because the drug is officially banned from use, athletes are using it on the sly. Since the drug needs to be injected. and needles and syringes can't be requisitioned from athletic departments athletes are sharing needles and becoming infected with AIDS and other communicable diseases.

There are no short cuts to success. You can't win if you don't play by the rules.

If you don't play by the rules now during your growing years, winning will become more and more difficult in your adult life.

Taking steroids is out of bounds. If your coach condones steroids, he condones cheating and messing around with your body's chemical make-up. You have to set your own standards and do what's right for you. You are accountable for your own actions.

Athletic events are over within hours, sometimes minutes. You'll have to live with the side effects of the drug for much longer. Even worse, you'll always know that you didn't make it on your own.

Summary

- [ ] Studies have shown that many high school athletes are still using anabolic steroids, some with the consent and help of their coaches.

- [ ] Coaches, teachers, doctors — any adults to whom you might look for advice — are human, too. They make mistakes of judgment; they don't always look out for your best interests.

- [ ] You must be the one to set the limits. Take responsibility for doing the right thing.

- [ ] Taking steroids can be dangerous, and sometimes fatal. No bona-fide scientific study has ever proved that steroids improve athletic performance.

- [ ] Reach beyond your grasp by playing fair and obeying the rules. It will make you a winner.

Note To Parents, Teachers and Counselors:

Western culture, especially American, places emphasis on competition. But at what cost? The emphasis is misplaced.

Participating fairly to the best of your capabilities and constantly working to improve those capabilities puts you in the winner's circle, no matter what the score.

Society promotes the idea that it's all right for underprivileged youth to push beyond acceptable limits in sports to escape poverty. Yet the number of high school students actually reaching the lofty professional ranks is much less than one percent.

Even for those who make it, the span of their wage-earning is short-lived. Because of that, John Thompson, basketball coach of Georgetown University, stresses the importance of education to his players. Ninety-eight percent of them graduate with a degree, giving them much more than just athletic "options."

Society needs to reinforce the concept of rewarding fair play and ethics. A clear goal must be set: The use of steroids is dangerous, illegal and will not be tolerated.

Random testing for usage before competition and mandatory testing during and after competition should be instituted. The technology is available and should be standardized and financed. Stiff penalties should be inflicted. Limits need to be re-established and kept.

Technology can provide tools to monitor athletic activities, but the basic belief of fair play must be instilled as a prime goal of achievement, rather than winning only by scoring high.

A great disparity exits between what school officials estimate steroid usage to be and what the students themselves say. School officials recently contended that only 6.6 percent of the student athletes are using steroids.

However, 68.7 percent of high school seniors admitted they had used them, often with the coaches' approval. That's more than 100 times the school officials' estimate.

Considering the serious consequences of taking steroids, 6.6 percent is a figure to merit concern. A hundred times that should trigger alarms.

But winning is so ingrained into our youth that many say they will not stop using steroids no matter what the side effects.

In fact 25 percent of steroid users said they would continue using them even if it were proven beyond a doubt that they caused liver cancer, heart attacks and sterility.

Plus, with many of the athletes sharing hypodermic needles, there is the added risk of contracting AIDS, syphilis and other diseases.

This is a behavorial problem. How can our youth rationalize such self-destructive behavor? Where did such convoluted values come from?

In women, taking steroids results in such "masculinizing" as hair growth, husky voices, oily skin, breasts becoming smaller and irregular menstruation.

Yet, when 10 women athletes participated in a study revealing their steroid use and its side effects, all 10 justified their usage on the grounds that it was necessary to win.

Even the distance runner Mary Decker Stanley is quoted as saying in the *Washington Post*, Jan. 16, '89 that performances will deteriorate if her sport cracks down on drugs. Notably, however, she favors stringent testing.

Why does America tolerate such destructive practices? One factor may be the question of whether or not setting limits in school can be taught to everyone.

Limits establishing values and the concept of right or wrong, fair play or foul, must be instilled in young people. The home and the church are good bases. High schools and colleges need to take a leadership role in this issue.

Society itself must clamp down on destructive behavior and corrupted goals. Young people are part of a community. A concentrated effort must be made to make them feel a part of this community to give them a sense of identity and belonging.

That way, they will be sensitive to what the community approves and, in turn, disapproves of. They will feel responsible to the community and be responsive to its needs, its spirit.

The community has a responsiblity to set priorities and establish the ground rules. Society can't go on worshiping wealth, gained at any price or fame bought by cheating and glory purchased with illegal aids.

Since the use of steroids is a behavorial problem, new direction must be given to change this behavior. Each adult can help change that direction, bolstered by the families, school, church, booster clubs — the entire community.

If you suspect a youth is using steroids, talk with him or her about it. Don't dodge the issue. Many athletes, coaches and even doctors deny that the use of steroids is harmful. Read up on it and see for yourself.

Become informed on steroids, before a new "epidemic" demolishes the health of our youth. Re-think your definition of "winning" and see if there's any room for breaking the law in it and causing health risks for our young people.

America with it's fixation on competing may be selling out its youth for a few high scores and coveted titles. The values of honest competition and fair play must be reinstilled. Those violating the rules need to be thrown out of the game.

Chapter 7

Setting Limits on Illicit Drug Use

If someone asked you to be a guinea pig in an experiment, you'd want to know what would happen to you. If you thought the effects would be harmful, you wouldn't hesitate to say no.

Don't experiement with drugs without knowing the facts. Be objective before you turn your body and mind into a war zone.

Our society has declared a war on drugs. A survey done by the *New York Times* and *CBS News* in 1988 found that 48 percent of the respondents — adults — named international drug traffic as Public Enemy Number One.

Young people often blame peer pressure for their drug use. It certainly exists, but there are limits to its effectiveness. If your peers asked you to jump off the top of the Sears Tower, would you do it?

Availability of drugs, peer pressure, having a disappointing family environment or being poor are all cop-outs for why anyone uses drugs.

The real reason for drug use lies in the character of the user. It's a matter of poor self-respect and wrong values.

Gaining protective self-esteem is the first step in avoiding drug use. That's what this book is all about.

Being knowledgeable about the effects of drugs on the human body is arming yourself with solid reasons for avoiding them.

Drugs: You either do them or you don't.

You either respect your body or you don't.

You value your own ability to reason and react, to interact with others, to find pleasure in healthy, happy — and legal — pursuits, or you don't.

You control your option.

Cocaine

In a national survey, 17.3 percent of high school seniors in the class of 1986 admitted to having tried cocaine. That was a two-fold increase over a similar study conducted in 1975.

Cocaine-related emergency room visits in 545 hospitals in 27 metropolitan areas increased from 5,000 in 1982 to 25,000 in 1985.

Because cocaine is illegal and highly addictive, there's no question that cocaine use has become a major drug problem in America today.

☐ What it is

√ Cocaine is a drug derived from the coca plant which grows in South America. It's a powerful stimulant that affects the central nervous, cardiovascular and sympathetic nervous systems.

√ Cocaine is commonly sold as a powder. It sells on the street for $75-100 per gram. You rarely, if ever, find pure cocaine. As it moves through the market, it is cut with other inactive ingredients.

√ Since there is no control over the manufacture and sale of cocaine, the average drug user has no way of knowing exactly what he or she is buying or using. It's not surprising that many cocaine-related medical emergencies involve cocaine that was improperly cut or contaminated with an even more deadly substance.

☐ How it's used

√ The most common way to use cocaine is by nasal inhalation or "snorting." Because it is water soluble, it can also be injected intravenously.

√ When mixed with another drug like an amphetamine, it is known as a "speedball." The effect of the drug is heightened, but so are the risks. *Saturday Night Live* comedian

---

All of this talk about drugs may lead you to think, "Sure, that's easy for you to say. You're a professional person, a physician, a teacher. You don't know what it's like to be a kid today!"

I spent my early childhood on the lower east side of Manhattan. The gangs used me as their mascot and good luck charm when I was only three years old. Drugs have always been readily available in New York. Many of my classmates used them. I was never sheltered from drugs.

John Belushi died of cardiac arrest after being injected
with this deadly concoction.

√   As a powder, cocaine can't be smoked. The heat deacti-
vates the drug. "Crack" is a smokable form of cocaine,
made by heating the powder with alkali salt and water.
It's available on the street in pieces resembling small
rocks. It sells for $5 to $10 per package.

Drug users either die or give it up so they can get on with their lives.

☐ Crack

√   Crack works on the body like
cocaine only faster. You feel
the high faster, you lose the
high faster, you become ad-
dicted faster.

☐ Ice

√   "Ice" is an even more lethal
form of smokable cocaine. Since first appearing on the
street just a few years ago, it has left a trail of death behind.

☐ The High

√   Cocaine first produces a sense of well-being, a euphoria
or "high." The high is short-lived and increasingly higher
levels of cocaine are necessary to maintain the high.

√   As dependency and tolerance increases, cocaine users are
led into a deadly booby trap. The body sends out signals
for more cocaine when actually it has absorbed all the cocaine it can use. This reaction is totally out of the user's
control and he or she is left with a craving more cocaine
cannot cure.

√   The incredible energy and warm feelings of security that a user gets from the initial cocaine high wear off, leaving chronic users suffering from depression, mood swings, memory loss, paranoia and aggressive behavior. They will be obsessed with cocaine and recapturing the high.

❐ The Side Effects

√   Insomnia
√   Nose bleeds
√   Tremors
√   Dry mouth and loss of appetite
√   Loss of sex drive
√   Cocaine use by pregnant women can result in birth defects and fetal drug addiction

❐ Toxic reactions

√   Convulsions
√   Dangerously elevated blood pressure
√   Repiratory failure, stroke and cardiac arrest
√   Death

❐ The Human Waste

Users give up control of their lives in exchange for a few minutes of pleasure. Chronic users put themselves on the level of Pavlov's dogs, not thinking but simply responding to physical stimuli. They lose interest in family, school and hobbies, further separating themselves from the responsibilites and rewards of everyday life.

Amphetamine

☐ What it is

√ Amphetamine, also called "speed," is a central nervous system stimulant and appetite depressant. It was used extensively as a diet pill until it was realized that its negative side effects far outweighed its benefits.

√ Amphetamine is available by prescription. It's also manufactured and sold illegally.

☐ The High

√ The user feels a sensation similar to a rush of adrenalin.
√ The user feels energized and the senses are heightened.

☐ The Side Effects

√ Increased blood pressure
√ Sweating and dry mouth
√ Hyperactivity
√ Cardiac and respiratory functions are stepped up — just as they would be if you suddenly found yourself standing on a highway in front of an oncoming truck.
√ Amphetamines are highly addictive. Tolerance is built up to the drug quickly, requiring higher dosages for the same effect.
√ Insomnia and a general state of agitation
√ Prolonged use can cause psychotic episodes and malnutrition. Existing tendencies toward anti-social or irrational behavior can be aggravated.
√ Withdrawal from the drug, even after short-term usage, can result in depression and fatigue.

The use of opium, an extract of the opium poppy, grown in the Far East and other are-

	Opiates

as of the world, has been documented for five thousand years. Its first recognized medical use was for gastroenteritis and diarrhea, and is still used in prescriptions for these ailments. Unlike cocaine and amphetamines, which are stimulants, opium and its derivatives are depressants. Opium, used as an illicit drug, is smoked, sniffed or taken orally. Smoking is preferred because of the instantaneous reaction.

❑ The Derivatives of Opium

√ **Morphine** is an effective but addictive pain killer used today in America, chiefly in the hospital setting. It is water soluble and can be administered by injection.

√ **Heroin** is synthesized from morphine. It is primarily an illegally manufactured street drug, much stronger in its effects. It is also water soluble and can be administered by injection.

√ **Codeine**, a milder derivative of opium, is used in prescriptions for pain relief and as a cough suppressant.

❑ The High

√ Opium and its derivatives act on the brain as an analgesic, deadening pain.
√ Opium and its derivatives produce a pleasant euphoria, generally without loss of consciousness.

❑ The Side Effects

√ Drowsiness and impaired motor skillls
√ Depression of the respiratory system
√ Female opium users experience menstrual cycle disruption

❏ Toxic reactions

√   High dosages can induce respiratory failure and death.
√   Opium abusers develop chronic hepatitis.
√   Babies born to opium abusers exhibit withdrawl symptoms, feeding difficulties and even convulsions.
√   Withdrawal from the drug during pregnancy can cause miscarriage or premature birth.

Addiction to this family of drugs seems to be one of the hardest addictions to kick. Your prognosis, if you're a young abuser, is poor. No matter what your odds for success, the best thing is to not get involved with opium in the first place.

Hallucinogens

Mescaline

Several years ago as a member of the Committee of the American Academy of Pediatrics on the American Indian and Alaskan Natives, I witnessed the use of peyote, a cactus plant containing mescaline, on an Indian reservation during a religious ritual. Certainly the reaction I observed was not of an extreme nature. Older cultures of Mexico, such as the Aztecs, used peyote in religious ceremonies. Mescaline is an illegal drug. Use of peyote is still permitted to certain American Indians for controlled use in their rituals.

❏ What it is

√   Mescaline is a psychedelic drug which acts on the sympathetic nervous system. It usually comes in capsule form.

❏ How it's used

√   It must be swallowed rather than smoked or injected. Effects are noted within one hour and last for half a day.

☐ The high

√ There are psychedelic effects, such as visual hallucinations, including designs in color.

☐ The side effects

√ Symptoms are similar to those for other stimulants: Increased blood pressure and body temperature, large pupils and excitability.

LSD (Lysergic Acid)

This is a most powerful hallucinogen first isolated and synthesized in the 1930s by Dr. Albert Hoffman at Sandoz Laboratories in Basel, Switzerland. The active product was lysergic acid. After a period of experimentation in the '50s, it was clearly documented as a psychedelic drug.

☐ What it is

√ The drug is easily dissolved and often sold on a piece of blotting paper (blotter acid), with effects beginning 40 to 60 minutes after ingestion. The effect lasts 8 to 12 hours with peak action at four hours. Below are some of the effects of LSD.

☐ The high

√ LSD — also called "acid" — alters your vision, distorting shapes and sizes of objects.
√ Bizarre acoustic distortions occur also, along with hallucinations. Tiredness sets in as the psychedelic effects wear off.

☐ The side effects

√ Frequent users develop tolerance to LSD.
√ It is not uncommon for users to experience recurrence of hallucinations — called flashbacks — even though usage of the drug has stopped.

√ Panic attacks while using the drug are common and can
  lead to psychosis which requires long-term treatment.
√ Irrational behavior when under the influence of LSD can
  lead to physical damage or suicide.
√ Overdoses of the drug can cause convulsions, coma with
  respiratory failure and death.

PCP (phencyclidine)

This anesthetic was introduced in the 1950s and heralded as a
pain-relieving, non-barbiturate, non-narcotic, intravenous agent.

It proved to have undesirable side effects, not the least of which
was hallucinations.

Use with humans was discontinued but is has continued to be
used for animal anesthesia by veterinarians. PCP appeared on the illicit drug market in the '60s.

Over the years, PCP has earned a reputation as a "bad trip" and
use has declined. A National Institute of Drug Abuse survey showed
that in 1986, no more than 12 percent of high school seniors had used
hallucinogens, probably PCP. Some characteristics and effects of
PCP follow.

☐ What it is

√ PCP is often mixed with parsley, poor-quality marijuana, or
  some other vegetable matter, and smoked.
√ It is also sold as a powder and infrequently as tablets. It can
  be eaten or snorted.
√ On the street, PCP is called "angel dust," "crystal," "elephant
  or horse tranquilizers" and "peace weed."
√ The drug's effects are felt within minutes of snorting or
  smoking and last for 15 to 30 minutes.
√ Ingested PCP works in 30 minutes and lasts two to five
  hours.

☐ The high

√ PCP causes mild hallucinations or perceptual distortions. The user appears to be "out in left field" or out of contact with reality. Higher doses produce stronger hallucinations.

☐ The side effects

√ Flushing and sweating
√ Rapid heart beat, heart irregularities and high blood pressure
√ Memory loss, numbness and coma
√ Rigid muscles, kidney failure and convulsions
√ Death
√ Newborn babies react similarly if the mother was a user up to three weeks before delivery.

Sedatives/hypnotics (depressants)

Sedative drugs often abused are barbiturates, methaqualone and glutethimide. Their use began in the 1700s but weren't widely prescribed until the 20th century.

In 1986, 10 percent of high school students admitted to long-term use of sedative/hypnotics.

√ **Methoqualone (Quaaludes or "ludes")** was introduced in the United States in1965 and became a major drug of abuse. It is now only manufactured illegally in this country.
√ Methaqualone and glutethimide ("goofballs") are nonbarbiturates.
√ Popular barbiturates are:
  • Phenobarbital ("reds")
  • Secobarbital ("reds")
  • Amobarbital ("blues) and
  • Pentobarbital ("yellow jackets")
√ The effects of all these drugs, barbiturate or not, are similar.
  • They are mood modifiers that work on the central nervous system.

- They mimic alcohol intoxication, including unsteady walking, slurred speech and poor muscle coordination.
- They all produce drowsiness eventually, although initial reaction may be excitement.
- Sedatives can be addictive with several months of use.
- Tolerance is developed, creating the need for higher doses to gain the desired effect.
- When taken in large doses, these drugs can cause coma.
- Withdrawal from sedatives is life-threatening and should be done under medical supervision.

√ **Tranquilizers** are probably the most widely prescribed and widely abused drugs in the world. Their abuse crosses all lines of society.

- **Meprobamate (Equanil, Miltown)** was introduced in the 1950s. It has a history of serious allergic reactions, including aplastic anemia.
  — Large doses can cause cardiac irregularities, coma and convulsions.
  — Withdrawal symptoms after heavy use are similar to barbiturate withdrawal and include seizure, coma and death.

- **Benzodiazepine (Valium)** is a powerful muscle relaxant. It is more effective than meprobamate and has superseded Miltown as the tranquilizer of choice for abusers since the 1960s. Side effects are:
  — dizziness, unsteadiness and sleepiness;
  — incorrect dosage can cause blurred vision and slurred speech;
  — mixed with alcohol, Valium's effects are potent and can cause hallucinations;
  — physical dependency is possible; and
  — after prolonged usage, withdrawal can result in insomnia, irritability, sweating, muscle spasms, rapid heart beat, confusion and in extreme cases convulsions.

The hemp plant (Cannabis sativa) grows everywhere but especially

Marijuana (cannabinoids)

well in tropical or temperate climates. While all parts of the plant contain psychoactive substances (cannabinoids), the highest concentrations are found in the flowering plant.

The use of marijuana has a documented trail that stretches back over 5,000 years and involves many civilizations, great and small.

In Virginia, as well as many other states, cannabis sativa was grown for nearly 200 years for medicinal use as well as for the hemp fiber, which was made into rope. Its use as a psychoactive was outlawed in this century and it gained enormous popularity during the 60s and 70s.

A safe drug?

You want to experiment with the only brain you have?

It is estimated that some 60 million Americans have tried marijuana. Among high school seniors in the U.S., 50 percent have used the drug at least once. Daily usage by high school seniors has declined from 11 percent in 1977, to 4 percent in '86.

Of all the street drugs, marijuana is most-often promoted as harmless. In the 1960s, many, including a professor at the Georgetown University School of Medicine argued that there were no chronic ill-effects from using marijuana.

Compared to LSD or heroin marijuana's effects are mild. But it is illegal and there are consequences associated with its use. Clearly evidence today suggests that long-term use may be harmful.

Read the facts and decide for yourself.

☐ The high

√ Marijuana, or "pot," can be eaten but smoking the drug provides the fastest high and is the most common way it's used. The peak effect occurs between 10 to 30 minutes after smoking and then tapers off over the next few hours.

√ The drug works on the central nervous system, changing moods, distorting time perception and cognitive abilities. Motor skills may be impaired. It may become difficult to organize thoughts. There are similarities to alcohol intoxication.

Want to live at the bottom of society? That's where drugs will take you.

√ Users feel an increased sense of well-being, euphoria and drowsiness. Spontaneous laughter or giggling is a common effect, along with acute hunger.

√ The effects of marijuana cause some users to lose touch with reality and feel alienated from themselves and their surroundings. Some suffer memory loss.

☐ The side effects

√ bloodshot eyes, increased heart rate and blood pressure;
√ weight gain;
√ delirium and hallucinations;
√ aggravation of asthma and bronchial allergies;
√ reduced respiratory function and a higher incidence of sinusitis and bronchitis in chronic users;
√ decrease in sperm count and sperm mobility in males; and interference with ovulation in females.
√ Tolerance occurs after several days of use. Discontinuing the drug can lead to irritability, decreased appetite, restlessness and insomnia.

√   The psychological effects of chronic marijuana use are serious and include:
  • loss of motivation and energy ;
  • inability to formulate goals and carry them out; eu-
    phoria, coupled with detachment from reality; and
  • school and work performance suffers.

We're beginning to see long-term effects surface in habitual users. Evidence now suggests that habitual use of marijuana may affect the immune system which protects our bodies from infection
and other diseases. Some studies show that marijuana use leads
to the use of other more deadly drugs.

Using marijuana may seem like the thing to do but it will leave
you "out" in left field when it comes to being a winner. You can
win a major battle by leaving it alone or having the courage to
stop using it.

In 1986, a report showed makeshift laboratories were produc-
ing synthetic versions of opi-

Designer Drugs

ates. These new designer drugs ("Ecstasy," "Eve") are cheaper and
more potent than the drugs they mimic.

Read about the effects of opiates in that section of this chapter.
While many drugs are produced illegally and subject to problems
of quality control, these designer drugs have a higher incidence of
problems than most.

There are reports of death and of one user who developed irre-
versible Parkinson's Disease.

Alcohol has a unique honor. It is the only intoxi-
cant that's been Ok'd by society.

Alcohol

For this sanction, society pays heavily. Alcohol use is involved
in 50 percent of all crimes and highway accidents. It causes the

deaths of 30,000 Americans each year and we pay $100 billion each year for alcohol rehabilitation.

☐ The effects of alcohol

√ Alcohol is a drug. It's a depressant, although small amounts initially produce a state of excitement.

√ Most drinkers experience euphoria.

√ After a state of intoxication is reached, the drinker becomes sleepy.

√ If drinking continues beyond intoxication, the drinker may pass out.

√ Drinkers really do become uninhibited. They often get out of control emotionally. The effects depend on the individual.

- Some people become quiet and lovable.
- Others become boisterous, argumentative and aggressive.
- Some become melancholy and moody.
- Still others go totally berserk.

You have so much to give this world. You can accomplish so much. Why waste your time — and your body — on drugs or alcohol.

√ Drinkers also become more careless and vulnerable but in their impaired state are unable to realize their lack of control. Reflexes and mental reactions are slowed and motor skills impaired. They make others vulnerable to their mistakes and drunken acts.

While alcohol is a legal drug for those of legal age, there are laws against public intoxication. Laws differ from state to state.

☐ Be smart about alcohol

√ Generally speaking, you will not be intoxicated if your liquor intake does not exceed one ounce of hard liquor, four ounces of wine or 12 ounces of beer in one hour. Your individual metabolism, weight and other factors greatly affect this rule of thumb. There are people who are legally drunk after one drink.

√ Food in the stomach slows down the impact of alcohol, which is why it's better not to drink on an empty stomach. Eating while you're drinking is a good idea.

√ Chronic drinkers develop a tolerance for alcohol. Alcohol is chemically addictive. Some people are genetically predisposed to alcohol dependency.

❑ What alcohol can do to your body

√ When physical dependency exists, withdrawal symptoms such as delirium tremens and hallucinations can develop. A heavy drinking binge without dependency can produce these same symptoms.

√ Acute intoxication actually poisons the body and destroys brain cells. It causes respiratory depression and can cause death.

√ Habitual use of alcohol adversely affects all the body's organs, lowers immunity to disease and can lead to the development of debilitating and fatal ailments like hepatitis and Alzheimer's Disease.

√ Alcohol can cause serious birth defects. Pregnant women should not drink.

❑ If you don't drink, don't start. . . if you do drink, you can get help

If you think drinking is the thing to do, sit in on an Alcoholics Anonymous or Alateen meeting (see the back of this book for more information on these groups). If you already have a drinking problem, decide to face it and contact one of these groups now. You are not alone.

Alcoholism is rampant among teenagers today. At AA or Alateen, you'll meet others who have been where you are and sometimes beyond. They don't judge. They describe what's happened to them, what works and they listen and help. They care.

If you are in a family situation where someone else is abusing alcohol, contact Alanon or Adult Children of Alcoholics. They will help you deal with the manipulation and guilt that alcoholics use against their families.

Learning not to be a victim of addiction — your own or someone else's — will help you cope with the situation while developing your own self-esteem. You'll find a life free from false highs and the inevitable, bottomless lows.

| **Tobacco** | In the 19th century, technology for curing tobacco leaf led to the production of an attractive, thin-papered, rolled cigarette. |

At the end of World War I, the 1920s erupted into free-for-all fun — the Roaring '20s. Authority and adult wisdom were questioned; youthful rebellion flourished. Hard liquor, then prohibited, went down gullets as fast as hemlines went up with "flapper" styles.

Cigarette sales doubled during this decade. Young men and women were depicted brazenly puffing away in the movies, newspapers and wherever this youth revolution was paraded.

Who could know then that this symbol of the flaming youth of the '20s would be responsible for so much death? Some 50 years later, the National Institute of Drug Abuse found that 362,000 people died as a result of smoking: 50 percent from heart and vascular disease, 36 percent from cancer and 17 percent from lung disease.

Nicotine from cigarettes is a primary cause of these killer diseases. The risk of death from coronary heart disease is five to 20 times greater if you're a smoker.

There are an estimated 30 million smokers today and nearly 10 million suffer from chronic bronchitis, emphysema and other lung problems related to smoking.

A burning cigarette releases nicotine into your body, along with other chemical compounds from the paper and tobacco. Some are documented carcinogens (cancer-causing agents).

☐ This is what tobacco does to your body

√ Nicotine can cause increased blood pressure and heart rate; it stimulates the intestinal tract, sometimes causing diarrhea. It also stimulates the brain. This can result in jitters, irritability or tremors.

√ Females who smoke have a higher incidence of stillbirths, miscarriages and underweight births.

√ Although nicotine is a stimulant, it reduces muscle tone, creating a feeling of relaxation. That effect causes many smokers to claim they smoke to relax.

√ Smoking is physically addictive and if you decide to stop, it's good to have professional advice and support. Some smokers find a gradual reduction in their intake of nicotine helps them quit; others prefer to go "cold turkey." Some find aids like *Nicorette* chewing gum helpful. There are seminars, video tapes and clinics, as well as your family physician who may be able to help.

☐ Quitting and Withdrawal

√ Withdrawal symptoms include insomnia, irritability (sometimes severe), headache, abdominal pain and craving.
√ When you stop smoking, it can take your body 6 to 10 years

to recover. After that time, your risk of death from most disease levels off only slightly above non-smokers. Destruction of lung tissue, however, is not reversible.

Caffeine

Caffeine is included in this writing, not because it's illegal for minors but to illustrate that too much of a good thing can cause problems. A little self-discipline needs to be used in forming good, rather than bad, habits. Caffeine is a stimulant and it can be addictive.

Coffee, tea, cocoa, chocolate and colas contain caffeine. Cocoa and chocolate also contain another stimulant, theobromine.

A cup of coffee contains 85 mg. of caffeine; tea, 50 mg.; and a cup of cocoa, 25 mg. A 12-ounce bottle of cola contains 50 mg.

☐ Physical Effects of Caffeine

√ It dilates blood vessels around the heart causing increased flow.

√ It narrows blood vessels to the brain.

√ It relaxes bronchial tubes and causes the kidneys to produce more urine.

√ Too much caffeine may cause anxiety, nervousness, rapid breathing and heart abnormalities.

√ Massive doses of caffeine can cause convulsions.

√ Pregnant women should stop their intake of caffeine. It can cause abnormal development and chromosome disorders in the fetus. Caffeine should also be avoided by nursing mothers — it passes through the breast milk and has a detrimental effect on the baby.

√ Caffeine may cause physical dependency. When you drink six to 10 cups of coffee a day, abstinence may result in headaches, discomfort and even depression.

Confining yourself to reasonable intake early will prevent some health problems plus possibly keep you from being restricted from caffeine all together later when you could really use an "eye opener" in the morning.

Summary

☐   Drugs are the number one problem in society. It's important to know their effects, the damage they do and to be able to recognize the symptoms.

☐   It's also important to wonder why ours is such an addictive society. Why do we think we need the effects of such chemicals? We scream in outrage over the thought of chemical warfare on the battlefield and then turn our bodies into chemical war zones.

☐   The physical consequences of drug use are serious and they're compounded when drugs are manufactured or processed for illicit street use. Street drugs are not always what they're said to be. Thousands of users become victims every year when they buy something far more potent than they bargained for or when drugs are contaminated or cut with seriously harmful additives.

☐   Even more serious are the psychological effects of drug use. Drug users have to live outside the law and beneath the standards of acceptable behavior in our society.

☐   Even if you can afford your drug habit and avoid becoming a thief, you will be a liar and a cheat. You can't be open about using illicit drugs; you won't be able to tell your family and friends who care about your well-being.

☐   Getting drugs and using drugs will become the most important thing in your life: more important than love or earning a living, more important than you. Every action, every plan will be predicated on maintaining your high.

☐   Even if you try to maintain a "normal" life and aspire to success and happiness, you will have to surround yourself with people who are losers. You will become what they are. It's inevitable.

☐   When you must lie to maintain your life, when chemical dependency rules you, when the most important people in your life are the losers who understand and feed your need for drugs, then you will have lost all self-respect and motivation to succeed.

☐   If you think you are different, that you can handle and control your drug habit alone, think again. Thousands of former addicts are living proof that it just won't happen. They can tell you stories of casual use that turned into nightmares of addiction. They had dreams, they thought they were different: they were just like you.

☐   There are numerous treatment programs and support groups for those with drug-use problems. Narcotics Anonymous, Alateen and other groups are listed along with their phone numbers at the back of this book.

☐   There are also support groups for those of you who want to "just say no" to drugs but are under pressure from peers and other circumstances.

☐   Whatever your situation, help is available: from trained professionals to young people who have faced the same problems and now want to help you overcome them.

☐   Read up on drugs and have the courage and intelligence to decide you don't need them. Get high on doing a job to the best of
your ability. Get high on the excitement of setting goals beyond
your reach and attaining them. Get high on life.

Note To Parents, Teachers and Counselors:

America is fighting a war daily, the War on Drugs. In April of
1988, a New York Times/CBS News poll asked: "Which of these five
international problems do you think is most important now: arms
control negotiations, terrorism, international drug traffic, Palestinian
unrest in Israel or Central America?"

Drug traffic was the overwhelming answer. Forty-eight percent of
the respondents named drug traffic as Public Enemy Number One.

In that same year, $2.5 billion was spent for interdiction, investiga-
tion, prosecutions, intelligence and other international drug activities. Despite record arrests of drug traffickers, only a small percent-
age of cocaine coming into this country was seized.

"Supply reduction has been an abject failure," said Dr. Lloyd Fa-
lueston, a social psychologist at the Institute for Social Research at
the University of Michigan who conducts an annual survey of drug
use by high school seniors.

The use of cocaine by high school seniors doubled during the 10
years from 1975 to 1985, from 5 percent to 10 percent, according to
surveys conducted by the National Institute of Drug Abuse, Survey
samples ranged from about 4,000 to 8,000.

During that same 10 years, the increase in population base was
less than 10 percent, yet cocaine usage doubled in the specified age
group.

Some blame availablity of the drug for the increase. Youth has a tendency to experiment and an ample supply of a drug can arouse curiosity in some. Yet, experimental usage alone does not account for a 200 percent increase.

The risk associated with experimental use is that the false sense of pleasure from the drug becomes a top priority daily. The user is no longer experimenting. He or she's hooked. He or she's now dependent.

Testing methods can identify cocaine usage 48 to 72 hours after use. Small amounts of cocaine are excreted in the urine. The blood and liver enzymes degrade cocaine.

Treatment works, but only for those who stay in the program. Only about 20 percent of those who need treatment are in these programs. Drug treatment centers need to be expanded and more workers trained for the centers due to the number of cocaine addicts.

Opiates are metabolized by the liver and are excreted via the urine within four hours. Urine tests can be positive for 48-96 hours after use.

Treatment is available for acute overdoses in emergency rooms. Young addicts have a poor long-term prognosis. Methadone detoxification is available but involves a week or more of abstinence.

Alternative programs include residing in drug-free communities for an extended time and methadone maintenance. The latter combines daily doses of a substitute narcotic with support services.

Use of PCP, benzodioze and meprobamate can be identified through urine tests. Treatment is available for the abuse of these drugs.

Blood testing for marijuana use is available and levels do correlate with exposure. Urine testing is available; for frequent users the test registers positive for several days. Metabolites of marijuana may be stored in fat tissue and can be detected weeks later.

Simply outlawing the use of marijuana isn't working. More comprehensive studies need to be made and publicized. Society — especially youth — needs to be educated about the dangers of marijuana.

Of all the drug problems that face teens today, alcoholism may be the most serious. Alcohol is easily available and, as adults, we don't always set good examples for its use. Young people may be dramatically affected by the alcoholism in their families or among friends, even if they don't drink themselves.

Make sure your young people know that there are support groups and treatment centers that can help them deal with alcohol addiction, whether it's their own or someone else's.

The drug problem must be a top priority for all. Usage now extends down into elementary school students. Communities and society as a whole must rise up against drug abuse.

Drugs are killing children. Drug traffickers are destroying our system of law. Babies are being born with severe deformities and limited mental capacities.

Long-term effects of drug usage in many instances are still unknown. What drugs our youth take today may affect future generations.

The cost of addiction is staggering. The cost to society in terms of crimes committed related to drugs and the rehabilitation of both prisoners and patients is astronomical. The Texas Department of Corrections estimates that 85 percent of the prisoners in its state facilities are incarcerated for drug-related crimes. The national average is close to that figure.

Job productivity has suffered from workers' drug usage.

The drug problem is certainly an international one with a high profit motive. Drug traffickers are pushing for bigger and bigger profits, a bigger market.

These profits are made easier with the support of countries that keep growing illegal plants for their own economic livelihood.

In the U.S., there is a growing demand for drugs as well as the money to support the illicit market. Our job individually is to work on the demand side.

Help youth find the self-esteem that keeps them from seeking the escapism of drugs. Participate in educational programs to alert them to the very real dangers of drug abuse. Watch for early warning signs so help may be obtained as quickly as possible.

The nations of this world somehow must come to grips with international monitoring, control and economic support for countries dependent on a high cash crop. Effective economic programs must replace crops that can kill.

The beginning of a truly successful War on Drugs is you and me, how we see society's role and how we can help youth cope with and conquer the real world, without drugs. And we need to see it both as a problem at home and as a world-wide problem in need of global resolution.

Chapter 8

Setting Limits on Sex

Talk about sex should ring a bell in any young person's mind. For your parents, it's usually an alarm bell. While this subject burns and smolders in the hearts and minds of everyone, few are willing to discuss it openly.

You're exposed to a lot of myths and misinformation concerning sex. These myths blow smoke around the nature, reason, need and most of all the responsibilities of human sexuality. Sex is fun, exciting and serious, all at the same time.

Sex is best with the right partner, and full knowledge of the subject.

Otherwise, it can be degrading and with AIDS out there dangerous.

Some would have us believe that sex is strictly for procreation. Like other creatures of the earth, we are programmed to procreate to keep our species going. The instinct to mate, to reproduce, is the strongest there is.

Today, with embryo transplants and artificial insemination, having sex is no longer needed for that, technically speaking. Even so, most couples prefer to have children the old fashioned way. Why? Because the sex act is enjoyable. It is true union between a man and a woman.

Being the highest level of life on earth, we try to set higher standards of behavior than just rutting around in the bushes. Because humankind has found that self-esteem and a little dignity add a great deal to life — and to sex — we try to assume responsibility for our acts and the outcome of those acts.

Having sex creates a physical and emotional reaction, positive or negative, sometimes both when we feel guilt or remorse about it. It does not leave us unaffected, that's for sure.

It creates a relationship, whether we want one or not, and it makes us look at ourselves differently because of this. It changes our relationship with ourselves even if the other person seems unaffected.

Many young people rush into sex because they want proof that someone loves them. A survey of young women in homes for unwed mothers turned up a constant theme: the girls had not wanted sex per se as much as they wanted to be held.

How do you keep from going too far when you're all steamed up?

When the sex glands take over, look out! The only solution may be not getting so hot to begin with. **Cool it!**

If you find you're becoming too "distracted":

- pour that energy into other outlets like sports;
- distract yourself from sex; and
- wear yourself out at something else.

It takes incredible self-control, but it can be done.

Sex: Whatever You Decide, Be Informed

Many young men in this liberated society have expressed fear at being pushed into sex by peers and by their girlfriends. "I'm not ready for it," they've told me time and time again.

Whether you decide to have sex because you're looking for love or peer approval — or merely for the physical enjoyment — the outcome is almost always the same. You'll find emptiness and the nagging suspicion that you've "sold out" something special for a quick fix that didn't work.

If you're a young man. . .
You may feel that trying to "score" enhances your macho image. That is probably one of the cruelest misconceptions that teenagers continue to be gullible enough to believe. In fact, it is nothing to be proud of, as most mature men and women will tell you.

If you're a young woman. . .
You may feel your role calls for playing the tease, arousing sexual interest and generally leading your boyfriend up to the point no return. You may not intend to be a "bad girl" but there's something exciting about leaving a guy ready to rocket.

Showing each other consideration and respecting the power of each other's natural sex drive is what it takes to keep things under control. You both must set limits. There's no self-respect for either of you when you behave with only your own fleeting enjoyment in mind.

It takes partnership to forestall sex, just as it takes a partner to have it. Choose your partners carefully.

There's More to Sex Than Just Physical Contact

Just because you are physically capable of having sex doesn't mean you can handle the emotions or the responsibilities. It can really mix you up; it can change your life more than you can imagine.

Over one million adolescents become pregnant each year. Unwanted pregnancies are just that. No matter what decisions are made regarding the future, things are never the same for those involved. Don't kid yourself. It's traumatic.

The Centers for Disease Control had 1419 reported cases of AIDS among teens by March 1990. That's only one percent of the total U.S. cases, but the number of teen cases is doubling every 14 months.

Condoms and birth control pills or other contraceptives — used as directed and together — can guard against disease and pregnancy.

But there's no pill for guilt and remorse.

Sex when you aren't in a position to be responsible for your actions creates tension: "What if they find out?" "What if I'm pregnant?" "What if I get AIDS?" That's heady stuff to have nagging at you.

If you even suspect that having sex will make you feel that you've let down your family and others who care about you and, most of all, yourself, don't do it.

If you choose to have sex, take precautions that will keep you from unwanted pregnancy or disease. These aren't rules that just apply to you, they apply to everyone, no matter what their age or social standing.

According to health officials, many teens have turned to anal intercourse as a means of "safe" sex. While it does eliminate risk of pregnancy, it places you at high risk for contracting AIDS, syphilis and other sexually-transmitted diseases. It's not safe by any stretch of the imagination.

The age-old cop-out is that a "spontaneous" sex is more moral than having condoms and spermicide and other contraceptives around "just in case." It's ridiculous. You aren't abiding by any high standards if the sex you have is unplanned. A fire is fire, whether it started with spontaneous combustion or somebody's match.

Is anal sex "safe sex"? I wouldn't bet on it.

Anal sex will prevent pregnancy — but you're still at risk to contract AIDS as well as other sexually transmitted diseases.

If you think that spontaneous sex is more moral, think about this:

- **What's moral about becoming an AIDS carrier and infecting anyone you have sex with years before you even know you have it?**

- **What's moral about bringing a baby into the world that you can't properly care for and nurture?**

- **What's moral about infecting your baby with AIDS when it is born?**

Either make up your mind to not have sex and stick to it, or keep protection on hand and use it when you do have sex. A typical adult double-standard? Not at all. It's your decision whether or not to have sex. You're the one setting the standards.

You're playing with fire if you're playing around with sex.

Sex drive is a natural energy. You can channel that energy in any direction you wish including those activities that build your skills as a winner.

The point is YOU have control and no one else.

Sex is not only a feeling of desire or a sense of satisfaction. It's energy, a true drive, a force.

Unless redirected by you, this energy naturally goes into the biological sex drive. It has to have an outlet. Conflicts will arise when what you perceive society expects of you differs from what your biological instincts tell you to do. Never forget that you can control it and use it to make yourself a winner.

Sexual energy is an integral part of life, both physically and as a motivational force. You can pour it into physical activities like playing football, running, dancing, biking and other forms of exercise. You can use it to excel in any chosen activity, be it selling goods and services, woodworking, mechanics, writing, painting, acting or getting high grades. It literally gets the adrenalin pumping.

Watch Out For the Common Myths About Sex and Love

One of the biggest myths in our society is "Love conquers all." T.V. and movies foist this off in the name of romance in the hopes of bringing big bucks at the box office. The Romance Rating never fails to find a big audience.

Yes, love is a great motivator. But it's actually two mature people working hard together who "conquer" difficulties and learn to cope with life and its responsibilities.

Another myth is, "And they lived happily ever after." Look around you. Look at the number of divorces. Yet those couples, too, were once in love. Most of them loved each other enough at one time to start families. Unfortunately, "romance" went down the tubes and just one of them is going to be raising that family full time.

Don't be duped by film fantasy versions. Tune into real life to decide what's romantic. Feeling "in love" is one thing. Notice that lasting love isn't self-centered. It doesn't "use" the other person for its own gain or pleasure. The sex act itself can be a part of love or apart from it.

Don't rush into sex until you have a clear picture of who you are, what you want out of life and out of a person you'd consider sharing your life with.

Set your standards of conduct high and you'll find someone who matches up. Set them low and you're liable to find yourself involved with a real loser.

The highest number of known cases involving sexually

Sexually Transmitted Disease

transmitted diseases is in young people 15 to 25 years old.

There's evidence that syphilis increases the risk of contracting AIDS and passing it on, especially through open, syphilitic sores. This could increase the spread of AIDS like wildfire, hitting the inner cities hardest.

Nearly one-fifth of all people with AIDS today are in their twenties. Since it can take as long as 10 years from the time of infection for symptoms to show up many — if not most — of those victims were infected as teenagers.

Besides AIDS, syphilis is rampant again. The syphilis rate for teens aged 15 to 19 has increased by 67 percent since 1985, according to the Centers for Disease Control (CDC).

Syphilis is now at its highest level in all age groups since World War II. Infection rates in Atlanta, Philadelphia and Washington, D.C., now rival those of the most impoverished parts of the Third World.

Contracting one sexually transmitted disease can lead to getting another, often more serious, one. Ignorance of the diseases and how they are spread is a main factor that puts teens 15 to 19 years old in the highest risk group for many of these diseases.

☐ AIDS
(Acquired Immune Deficiency Syndrome)

AIDS, transmitted primarily by anal sex, is laying waste to the homosexual community. It's being spread by dirty needles used by drug addicts. It's spreading quickly to the rest of the population. The best way to protect yourself from this killer is to be informed and act accordingly.

√ AIDS is caused by the human immunodeficiency virus (HIV).

√ Within three weeks of HIV exposure, symptoms of acute infection may appear, such as fever, swollen glands, tiredness and flu-like symptoms. After the initial period of infection, symptoms disappear.

√ The symptoms may reappear after a period of time. It is believed that one-third of these victims will develop AIDS within six years.

√ In the more advanced stage of HIV infection, the victim develops the AIDS related complex (ARC). Symptoms include: weight loss, fever and diarrhea without obvious cause. Some of these victims may have neurological problems such as nerve weakness and not be able to think clearly due to brain dysfunction.

√ The AIDS virus attacks the T-4 lymphocytes in the body's immune system. The virus spreads from cell to cell, finally destroying the immune system. In this defenseless state, many victims die from illnesses such as pneumonia or cancer, or waste away from the ravages of AIDS.

√ The medical world is frantically searching for a way to stop and to cure AIDS. It has reached pandemic levels world wide. It is a killer. Treatment recently has demonstrated that AZT (Zidovudine) is effective in suppressing clinical symptoms in AIDS patients. Many drugs are being used experimentally but to date no cure is available.

√ AIDS is especially difficult to pinpoint. Following infection, it takes four to six weeks to show positive in a test, more so in some

If you think that you can't get AIDS, think about this:

√ **Can you be sure your sexual partner is safe?**
√ **Is he or she a virgin?**
√ **Even if he or she has only one other sexual episode, that person may have had sexual contact with someone else and so on down the line — there is a real "chain link" effect.**
√ **What if one of those links were bisexual?**
√ **What if they did drugs intravenously?**
√ **What if they slept with someone else who did?**
√ **What if they were given the AIDS virus in an unscreened blood transfusion years ago, or exposed to it through some other means?**

If you have symptoms and have reason to believe you may have contracted the virus, stop sexual activities and be tested. The AIDS Hotline phone number is listed in the back of the book.

cases. It may take as long as three months from the initial date of contact for the infection to show up.

√ The test — either the ELISA assay or the Western Blot assay — is not for the AIDS virus itself, but for the antibody the body develops against AIDS. Therefore, a positive result does not mean the person will absolutely develop AIDS. It does mean the person has been exposed to the virus.

√ On the other hand, a negative test does not guarantee that a person is free of the virus. False results are possible, as with any test, so follow-up tests are required for accuracy.

√ Because in the early stages of AIDS symptoms come and go, it is important to be tested if the initial symptoms appear.

√ Public health clinics will do confidential testing (a simple blood test) free or for a minimum charge.

√ These clinics are listed under the state or county government headings in the phone book. Counseling centers and private doctors are available to discuss the tests and further procedures.

Historically, virginity has been prized as an indication of honor and integrity. With AIDS, it may become one of the most valued commodities on earth.

√ Private test centers are listed in the back of the phone book (usually under medical laboratories), but do charge a fee.

√ If your behavior is putting you at risk, stop. If you are still a virgin,

The old idea of "saving yourself" for the right person may be back in vogue. While maintaining a chaste life isn't easy, no one ever died of it.

consider what having sex means in terms of this deadly epidemic. If you are going to continue to take risks, make them as safe as possible.

Only two virgins who don't do drugs can come together knowing they are truly practicing "safe sex" and that their children will be born AIDS-free. Think about that before giving up your virginity.

☐ Syphilis

There are some 35,000 cases of syphilis reported each year.

The highest incidence is in those ages 15-21. The biggest increase among teenagers during the 1980s was in black females aged 15 to 19. The infection rate in blacks has jumped 132 percent since 1985. Again, read the facts and be informed.

√ The disease is due to the bacteria Treponema pallidum.

√ It enters through the lining of the gential organs or breaks in the skin.

The symptoms are important to recognize since lack of treatment can lead to successive stages involving multiple vital organs and can cause dementia in the central nervous system. In other words, it can make you crazy — truly insane.

√ Syphilis starts with a chancre, or ulcer-like sore. It can appear on the penis, lips, mouth, face, neck or anus. The incubation period from time of infection to when the sore shows up is 10 to 90 days. The chancre is single, firm and not painful unless infected. It heals in three to six weeks.

√ The sore contains bacteria which can be identified in tests after six weeks; the sores may last two to 12 weeks. Following the chancre, there is a second phase which includes: itchiness of the skin, sore throat, headache and fever accompanied by rash on the palms of the hands and soles of the feet.

√ There are other generalized symptoms involving bones, the lining of the nose, eyes, liver, lymph nodes, gastrointestinal tract, lungs, kidney, spleen and blood. If untreated, the secondary phase disappears in four to eight weeks.

√ The later stages of syphilis are devasting to the brain, spinal cord, bones, heart and blood vessels.

√ A mother can transmit the disease to her infant as congenital syphilis. The infant may seem normal for several weeks and then general symptoms such as fever, anemia and failure to grow may appear. Pediatricians can diagnose congenital syphilis from tell-tale signs such as severe running nose, sores (lesions) in the lining of the mouth, anus and genitals.

√ Untreated congenital syphilis subsides but the organism lives in the body's tissues for some 50-60 years.

√ The child may have signs of the disease such as flat bridge of nose, high forehead, scars around the mouth and chin. With the appearance of first permanent incisors, there is a visible notch.

√ As mentioned before, the spyhilitic sores can make the victim more susceptible to contracting AIDS.

☐ Chancroid

This ulcer of the genitals is not caused by Treponema pallidum, which carries syphilis, but by Hemophilus ducreyi. The incubation period is three to five days. The early sore contains pus, then ulcerates. Local glands swell.

☐ Herpes

√ As much as 10 percent of the population is said to be infected with genital herpes. The cause is a virus which is classified with other viral infections, such as chicken pox.

√ In the male, genital herpes shows a blister-like lesion on the head of the penis, the glans. The blisters may be mutiple on the foreskin and shaft.

√ In the female, the lesions appear on the lips of the vagina, sometimes in the vagina, and on the buttocks.

√ These blisters are painful; they heal in one or two weeks. Associated with these blisters may be urinary symptoms, such as burning when urinating, fever and general malaise.

√ In cases where anal sex is practiced, rectal lesions are accompanied by rectal burning with defecation and constipation.

√ Therapy is available with medical consultation. The drug acyclovir has helped produce healing of the lesions and lessening of the pain. When the lesions are recurrent, therapy may not be as promising.

√ There is no cure for herpes. It is more contagious when blisters, which come and go, are present.

√ Undiagnosed herpes during pregnancy is a serious threat. The virus can cause miscarriage and stillbirth and can damage infants during birth. Caesarean sections are performed if the virus is active.

☐ Chlamydia

This is probably the most common baterical sexually transmitted disease and is a serious threat to teens. Left untreated, it can result in sterility both in females and males. Girls 15 to 19 appear to have the highest infection rate.

√ Chlamydia is difficult to detect as it has no overt symptoms. In women it can cause abdominal pain, nausea and low fever. In men it causes a discharge from the penis or painful urination.

√ In women, the infection usually begins in the cervix and spreads to the fallopian tubes or ovaries, causing pelvic inflamation, a leading cause of sterility.

√ The Centers for Disease Control (CDC) reports that in various areas of the U.S. between seven and 40 percent of female teens have been infected.

√ Many women ignore the symptoms only to find that later when they want to have children, they are not able to do so.

☐ Lymphogranuloma venerum

This is a condition with painless ulcers of the genitalia with associated enlarged glands caused by chlamydia trachomata. If left untreated, these glands become large and tend to ulcerate.

Medical treatment is available. Antibiotic therapy, such as tetracycline, sulfisoxazole and ampicillin, may be effective.

☐ Gonorrhea

Gonorrhea is an infection of the lining of the genital organs, known as the "clap," contracted by having sexual intercourse with an infected partner.

√ The organism can infect joints, bones, skin, heart and the lining of the central nervous system.

√ The incubation period is three to five days. Males show a yellowish discharge from the penis and females experience a discharge from the vagina, itching and burning during urination.

√ As many as one-third of all female cases may have no identifiable symptoms and it is now believed that some males may be asymptomatic as well.

√ Mothers infected with gonorrhea can give their babies ophthalmia neonatum, a disease which affects the baby's eyes, at birth. The bacteria can spread throughout the baby's body and cause meningitis and death.

√ Medical treatment is available. Penicillin can control most strains of N. gonorrhea. However, a cure does not provide immunity against this disease.

√ Mainly because of a nationwide control progam started in the '70s, the number of cases in teens has declined significantly according to CDC.

√ But CDC also reports that the rate of gonorrhea in black teenagers increased in the '80s. By 1988, the numbers of young blacks reported with the disease were 20 to 40 times higher than those of white teens.

☐ Urethritis

Non-gonorrhea urethritis is due to organisms other than GC, such as chlamydia trachomatis. This infection is like gonorrhea and is considered twice as common. Symptoms are similar: burning upon urinating, itchiness around the genitals and a discharge from the uretha. The disease can be without symptoms.

Medical treatment is available and tetracycline is effective.

☐ Gonorrhea inquinale

Painless lesions develop beneath the skin around the glands surrounding the genitals. These glands can ulcerate and cause constriction of the vagina or rectum. The organism causing this is a coccobacillus and responds to antibiotic treatment with tetracycline.

☐ Trichomonas vaginitis

This infection is caused by a protozoa organism. The discharge is foul smelling and can be frothy, white or yellow. Frequently the urethral opening may be red and swollen, causing painful intercourse. It can be reoccurring. Both partners require treatment.

☐ Hepatitis

This virus causes a serious liver inflamation and is highly contagious. Homosexuals and drug addicts have a high rate of infection. Blood and body fluids can transmit the hepatitis viruses A and B. Any break in the lining of the oral, genital or anal tracts can allow for the entry of contaminated fluids.

Symptoms include jaundice (the skin color turning yellowish) and the urine turning a dark, cola color. Medical treatment is needed.

☐ Mononucleosis

The so-called "kissing disease" is caused by the Epstein Barr virus of the herpes family. It lodges in the mouth and throat and lies dormant in the cells. It can be transmitted by kissing.

With stress, infection or trauma, a flare-up occurs. Fainting, tiredness, dehydration, swollen lymph glands and spleen are symptoms. Left untreated, it can cause serious problems and require a long period of rest to recuperate.

It is highly contagious. Many teens, especially those suffering from fatigue, are susceptible to it.

In Africa, this virus has been associated with tumors of lymph glands (Burkitt's lymphoma).

☐ Lice

Lice, commonly called crabs, can be a hazard of sexual intercourse and are usually found between the pubic hairs. The patient may itch and develop a rash. Medication (denzohexachloride) is available at drugstores.

☐ Genital warts

A virus can cause small warts on the genitals. They're usually painless but can itch. As many as one-third of all sexually active teens have them.

They are not considered dangerous unless their growth threatens to block body openings. However, doctors are concerned about an apparent connection between genital warts and cervical cancer that's not fully understood yet.

They can be removed, although some return, and sometimes they disappear on their own. If you have any and they worry you, the next time you have a physical or visit a doctor have them checked out.

As you can see, sex can involve everything

Finding the Right Set of Limits

from deadly disease to worrisome warts. If you are going to engage in sex, protect yourself and your partner.

If you have the courage and fortitude to remain chaste, you're in good company.

There's been much talk about the idea that sex is okay as long as it's between two consenting adults. Don't get your logic turned around and jump to the conclusion that if you consent to have sex then you must be an adult. Being adult has its privileges, but it also has its responsibilities.

Adults are just as susceptible as you are to sexually-transmitted diseases and unwanted pregnancies. Their actions can be disapproved by society and their peers.

A key word in this matter is responsibility. Most adults are at least financially responsible for the outcome of their acts. If they contract a disease, many have insurance to cover the cost of medical treatment. They have an income with which to pay the expenses that aren't covered. Most are financially responsible for babies their actions help create.

Having sex doesn't make you an adult. You are still a minor in the eyes of the law until you reach legal age. Until, at least, you can take economic responsibility for your actions, you are still a dependent.

If you're using sex to get even with your family for an unhappy home life, hoping for pregnancy to force your boyfriend or girlfriend into marrying you, you need to stop and think carefully about what you are doing.

Creating new problems doesn't solve the old ones. Strength of character and peace with yourself come only through finding the solutions to deal with life as it comes to us. Reach out for constructive help. It's there, waiting for those who need a hand to stay within their limits to become winners.

Summary

☐   Millions of teens, and even preteens, are sexually active. That doesn't make it the right thing to do. You need to know the dangers — emotional and physical — of sex. Sexually transmitted diseases are a real threat.

☐   You need to understand what a strong force the sex drive is, and how you can channel its energy into worthwhile activities.

☐   Young couples, out of mutual concern and respect, need to set limits and stick to them. "Saving yourself" for the right person has new validity in the face of diseases such as AIDS.

☐   If you decide to have sex, you need to use the protection of condoms and birth control agents containing spermicide, which also seems to help in fighting infection from the HIV virus.

☐   You're making the decision whether or not to have sex. You are setting your own standards. The decision of whether or not to use protection, which also happens to be birth control measures, is also yours. But you need to be aware of the possible consequences if you do decide to have sex and do not take precautions.

☐   Parents, peer groups, role models and the church influence your standards and decisions. Society can support moral conduct and condemn what it deems immoral. But it is ultimately each person's personal decision. It should be based on knowledge.

Note To Parents, Teachers and Counselors:

The culture we live in seems to have a forum controlled by those of unmatched intellect looking out for the benefit of humankind. Thus we have these high cultural plains giving us explicit sex action on T.V., from "soaps" to music videos.

Here's where young people (and children) can get graphic information about sex — the great mystery of life. Terrific. Why can't adults open up on this subject rather than entrusting Hollywood with it?

Although about 93 percent of U.S. high schools have some form of sex education, a lot must be flunking the course. Or doing their own research outside the classroom.

In metropolitan areas, studies show that 34 percent of girls and 50 percent of boys have had sex by age 16.

Studies show that nationwide, 50 percent of high school seniors in 1989 have had sex before graduation.

The article doesn't indicate whether or not it was "safe" sex, however 1.2 million adolescents are pregnant annually. Yes, attitudes about sex certainly are changing each year.

If, for some reason, there were an outbreak of polio again, you would immediately talk with your children, your charges and inform them of what it is, what it does, how it's caught and what to do to take precautions to avoid it.

You would try to help them set limits to keep from contracting it. You would set a good example yourself for them to follow to avoid infection.

Polio is caused by a virus. So is AIDS.

There's a vaccine to protect against polio. There's no vaccine or cure for AIDS.

Why can adults discuss in detail one type of disease, but hestitate to discuss one that is sexually transmitted? Somehow, parents and society must stop treating sex as a taboo subject.

Its powerful, natural drive must be acknowledged. Then youth can be shown constructive ways to control or divert their urges. But sex is a health issue. With AIDS, it's a crucial issue.

AIDS leaves a lethal legacy. According to the National Commission on Infant Mortality there are an estimated 20,000 cases of HIV-infected children in this country.

Most babies are infected by the mother at birth. It is possible the virus can be transmitted through breast milk. Not all infants born to mothers with AIDS are infected but may have the presence of antibodies passed on from the mother. These antibodies disappear between 12 months and 18 months of age.

Four to 5 percent of pregnant women in some inner city clinics test positive for HIV. Twenty to 60 percent of these mothers transmit the virus to their newborns.

In New York City, one in every 61 babies born tests positive at birth. Most of these children die of HIV-related diseases before the age of three.

Infants born with HIV have unique needs, especially if responsibile parents are unavailable. Long-term hospitalization is a drain on medical funds and there is always the possibility that these infants have other sexually transmitted diseases requiring treatment.

Older children require constant treatment for diseases associated with HIV immune supression. These diseases are of an infectious nature: tumors and chronic, lingering infections.

While teenagers comprise one percent of all reported cases of AIDS nationally, the screening results in Baltimore City health clinics is 1.5 to 2 percent. Data for the Department of Defense shows a one in 400 rate in the District of Columbia.

While the disease first surfaced in homosexuals and drug users, more women are becoming infected with the greatest incidence occuring in black and Hispanic populations, accounting for 51 percent and 21 percent, respectively, of all women with AIDS.

Most adults find discussing sex and sexual diseases terribly embarrassing. Somehow a way to discuss these subjects in a manner that lets both adults and young people retain their dignity must be found. Usually discussing it matter of factly accomplishes this.

But there can be no receptive discussion if the young person feels his or her behavior is going to be condemned or if he feels he is being grilled to see if he or she's been doing something wrong.

The discussion can't be judgmental.

It can be followed by the adult's expressing what he or she hopes the young person will do and a frank discussion of whether the youth feels he or she can live up to it and the problems in doing so.

Support is needed for a young person to hold fast to high standards.

Adults need to acknowledge that setting sexual limits and sticking with them are extremely difficult, but point out the alternatives. Find out what you can do to bolster your child's resolve.

Ignoring the high incidence of teenage sexual activity and teen pregancies isn't going to change it. Children are not only having babies, they're having babies infected with AIDS, syphilis and other tragic diseases.

Left to their own ingenuity, teens are now practicing high-risk anal intercourse to avoid pregnancy. They've gone from the frying pan into the fire. Sex education about these diseases is desperately needed, especially in the home on a one-on-one basis.

Don't let Hollywood be the one to shape your child's ideas on romance, love and sex. Communicate with them about a realistic view of love and sex.

Talk to them about couples who have solid relationships and how they manage it. Talk to them objectively about couples who have failed in their relationships and why.

If your own relationship has failed, be fair in your analysis of what caused it. If adults can't learn from past mistakes or to have any credibility with them how can we expect children to?

What does your sexual conduct say to your children? Do you practice what you preach? If you don't, can you give them a reasonable explanation of why you want them to act differently without getting defensive?

Let's drop the Victorian idea of "nice people don't do it — or at least they don't talk about it" and acknowledge that, with few exceptions, everybody does it because it is a natural instinct — and take it from there.

Nothing's more personal than a person's sex life. But having sex has become life-threatening. Take charge of your child's welfare. Talk with them, help them become informed. Give them feasible guidelines and values.

See that they read this chapter and have a heart-to-heart talk with them about it. Ask them questions and let them question you. See if it jibes with what they've heard or believe. Discuss whatever bothers them.

Although young people are sexually active, many are pitifully ignorant of the facts. Some may know a great deal more than you imagine. But can they relate the facts to themselves and figure out what to do about their social life and sexual conduct?

Seek out additional books, programs and speakers who talk the kids' same language. We all might learn something from them.

Help promote education, especially if you are a member of a minority group hard hit by these diseases. With the alarming rise in incidences of AIDS and syphilis, particularly in black and Hispanic teens, we may be seeing races unkowningly committing a form of genocide, or geno-suicide.

Your children and the youth of the world are at stake.

As one health official who works with pre-teens and teens put it: When it comes to diseases like AIDS, right now the only "cure" is education.

Resources for Information and Support Groups

As a young person today, you are confronted with many decisions which will affect the rest of your life. Below are some sources of information that will help you make informed decisions.

Alcoholics Anonymous (AA), Al-Anon, Alateen and **Adult Children of Alcoholics** carry phone listings of local chapters in either the white or yellow pages of the phone book. Or check with the local health department.

National Institute on Drug Abuse: 1-800-662-HELP (662-4357)

Narcotics Anonymous (NA) has a toll-free hotline: 1-800-777-1515

National Cocaine Hotline: 1-800-COCAINE

FACTS: 1-800-537-2287

AIDS Hotline: 1-800-342-2437

Sexually Transmitted Diseases Hotline (STD): 1-800-227-8922

Suicide Prevention Hotline: 1-800-767-5433

Suicide National Hotline: 1-800-333-4444

National Child Abuse Hotline: 1-800-422-4453

National Runaway Hotline (crisis and referrals): 1-800-231-6946

National Runaway Switchboard (counseling and shelter): 1-800-621-4000

Parent Alert System: 1-800-537-4774

Domestic Violence Hotline: 1-800-333-7233

Parent Resources Inst. (PRIDE): 1-800-241-7946

RespecTeen: 1-800-888-3820; offers a program sponsored by the Lutheran Brotherhood to help parents help their teens surmount the challenges of youth. Call the 1-800 number for more information and a free RespecTeen booklet, "Our Families . . . Our Future."

Planned Parenthood: 1-800-438-1019

Hotlines can answer questions, send you information, refer you to testing centers and support groups and so forth.

The AIDS Hotline volunteers cannot do individual counseling over the phone but can answer many questions and give excellent referrals. The STD Hotline is most helpful, can provide numerous referrals and their staff is easy to talk with, although they cannot do technical counseling.

NA Hotline can refer drug abusers to both open and closed (abuser only) meetings, recovery houses or have someone return the call if a crisis exists or the caller desperately needs to talk to someone. Such calls are done on a first-name basis only.

The National Institute on Drug Abuse also deals with those having drug or alcohol problems and is a treatment and referral hotline.

AA and most of the other support groups related to alcohol problems provide both referral information and someone to talk to about your problem.

If you get a busy signal for the hotlines, keep trying. You're not alone with your problem. Others are seeking help also. Most hotlines operate on a 24-hour basis.

The phone book, the library, schools, churches and public health departments are good sources for referral information.

References

ABC, T.V. Barbara Walters' program on high school student performances, Oct. 1988.

American Medical Association, *Drugs Used in Other Mental Disorders*, Drug Evaluations, 6th Edition, Chicago, AMA, p. 157, 1986.

Ancient China, Shafer, E.H., Time, Incorporated, 1967.

Atkinson, J.W., and Raynor, J.O, *Personality Motivation and Achievement*, with contributions by David Birch and Martina Souretis Horner. Hemisphere Publishing Corporation, New York.

Bakwin, H., M.D., and Bakwin, R.M., M.D., *Clinical Management of Behavioral Disorders in Children*, W.B. Saunders Co., Philadelphia, Pennsylvania, 1966.

Barr, M.L., and Bertram, E.G., *A Morphological Distinction Between Neurons of the Male and Female and the Behavior of the Molecular Nuclear Satellite During Accelerated Nucleoprotein Synthesis*, Nature, 1949, 163-676-677.

Camp, M. *Social and Personality Development*. Holt, Rinehart and Winston, New York.

Classical Greece, Bowra, C.A.A., Time, Incorporated, 1965

Creativity in Statecraft. Arthur Schlesinger, Jr., Library of Congress, 1983.

Creativity: A Continuous Inventory of Knowledge, The Council of Scholars, Library of Congress, Washington, D.C., 1981.

Diagnosis and Management of the Fetus and Neonate at Risk, Babson, S.G., Dervoll, M.D., and Benda, G.I. the C.V. Mosby Co., St. Louis — Toronto — London, 1980.

Early Islam, Stewart, D., Time, Incorporated, 1967.

Education Clearing House Task Force Report, Board of Trade, 1988.

Education Report, Board of Trade, December, 1987.

Gillman, A.G., Goodman, L.S., Rall, T.W., and Muran, I., *The Pharmacological Basis of Therapeutics,* 7th Edition, 1985, MacMillan Publishing Company, New York, NY 10022.

Hetherington, E.M., "Effects of Parental Absence on Sex-typed Behavior in Negro and White Preadolescent Males", *Journal of Abnormal and Science Psychology.* 4: 87-91, 1966.

Hull, David L., *Science as a Process,* The University of Chicago Press, 1988.

Hunt, A., Jones, R.T.," Tolerance and Dispostion of Tetrahydrocannabinol in Man", *J. Pharmacol. Ex. Ther.* 215, 35 - 46, 1980.

Imperial Rome, Hadas, M., Time, Incorporated, 1965.

International Congress on Drug Abuse, Georgetown University, November 14 - 16, 1988, Washington, D.C.

Isikoff, M. "Fighting the Drug War: From Arizona to Fairfax", *Washington Post,* November 6, 1988.

Jacobs, P., Brenton, M., Melville, M., Brittain, R., and McClemont, W., "Aggressive Behavior, Mental Subnormality and the XYY Male", *Nature*, 1965: 208, 1351 - 1353.

Janda, LL.H., and Klenke-Hamel, K.E., *Human Sexuality*, D. Van Nostrand Co., New York, 1980.

Jarik, M.E., "Biological Factors Underlying the Smoking Habit," *Research on Smoking Behavior*. National Institute of Drug Abuse, Washington, D.C., pp 122-146, 1977.

Johnson, L.D., O'Malley, P.M. and Bachman, J.G., *Drug Use by High School Seniors*, Class of 1986, U.S. Department of Health and Human Services, Pub. # ADM 87-1535, Rockville, MD 1987.

Julien, R.M., M.D., *A Primer of Drug Action*, 5th Ed., P. 179, 1988, W.H. Freeman and Company, New York.

Kinsey, A., Pomeroy, W.B., and Martin, C.E., *Sexual Behavior in the Human Male*, W.B. Saunders, Philadelphia, 1948.

Kinsey, A., Pomeroy, W.B., and Martin, C.E., *Sexual Behavior in the Human Female*, W.B. Saunders, Philadelphia, 1953.

LeCizoy, C.W., *Parent-adolescent Intimacy: Impact on Adolescent Functioning*. Adolescence, Spring, Vol. 2, 1988.

Lombardi, Vince, speech, "Habit of Winning."

Madden, J.D., Chappel, J.N., Zuspan, F., et. al., "Observation and Treatment of Neonatal Narcotic Withdrawal", *Am. J. Obstet. Gynecol.*, 127: 199-201, 1977.

Masters, W. and Johnson, V., *Human Sexual Response*, Little Brown, Boston, 1966.

Neinan, G. and Zeidner, M. "Effect of Decision Control on State Anxiety and Achievement", *Personality and Individual Difference*, Vol. 8, 1987.

Novello, J.R., M.D. *Bringing Up Kids, American Style*, A & W Publisher, Inc. New York.

Polin, W., *Research on Smoking Behavior*, Washington, D.C., 1977.

Rise of Russia, Wallace, R., Time, Incorporated, 1967.

Shearin, R.B., and Wientzen, R.L., *Clinical Adolescent Medicine*, G.K. Hall Medical Publishers, Boston, 1983.

Shervette, R.E., Schydlower, M. and Lampe, R.M., et. al.,"Jimson "Loco" Weed Abuse in Adolescents", *Pediatrics*, 63: 520-523, 1979.

Silber, T.J., Josefson, M., Hicks, J.M., et. al., Prevalence of PCP Use Among Adolescent Marijuana Users, *J. Pediatr.*, 112: 872-879, 1968.

Sound and Hearing, UFE Science Library, S.S. Stevens and Fred Warshofsky, Time, Incorporated, 1965.

Srivastava, P., and Singh, R. Age And Task Differences In Reduction Of Performance From Motivation And Anxiety Formation, *Child Development*, June, 1988.

Substance Abuse: A Guide for Health Professionals, Editor, Schonberg, S.E., p. 128, 1988, American Academy of Pediatrics. Pacific Institute for Research Evaluation.

Surgeon General Office of Smoking and Health. Department of Health, Education and Welfare Publication, Washington, D.C., 1979.

Tashkin, D.P., Calvarese, B.M., Simmons, et. al. "Respiratory Status of Seventy-Four Habitual Marijuana Smokers", *Chest*, 78: 699-706, 1980.

"The Alarm Response", Hans Selye, *Handbook of Physiology,* American Physiological Society, Washington, D.C. 1962.

The Changing Cigarette Health Consequences of Smoking, A Report of the Surgeon General, U.S. Department of Health and Human Services, Washington, D.C. 1981.

The Winning Horseplayer, Andrew W. Beyer, Houghton Mifflin Co., Boston, 1983.

The World of Michelangelo 1474 - 1564, Robert Coughlan and Editors of Time-Life Books, Time, Incorporated, New York, 1966.

Theories of Criticism, Abrams, M.H. and Ackerman, J., Library of Congress, Washington, D.C. 1984.

U.S. Department of Health, Education and Welfare, Alcohol and Health, Washington, D.C., 1978.

Watkins, J.D., *Report of the Presidential Commission on Human Immunodeficiency Viral Epidemic.*

"Wake Up America! We're Wasting Our Future", H. Ross Perot, *Washington Post,* November 20, 1988.

When It Comes to Education, Greater Washington Means Business, Board of Trade, April 1987.

Wiggins, J.D. Self-esteem, Earned Grades, And Television Viewing Habits Of Students High School Counselors. November, 1987.

Ziporyn, T., A Growing Industry and Menace: Makeshift Laboratory Designer.